Mary Seacole

D0493520

Mary Seacole

Ron Ramdin

HAUS PUBLISHING • LONDON

First published in Great Britain in 2005 by
Haus Publishing Limited
26 Cadogan Court
London SW3 3BX

Copyright © Ron Ramdin, 2005

The moral right of the author has been asserted

A CIP catalogue record for this book
is available from the British Library

ISBN 1-904950-03-5 (paperback)

Designed and typeset in Garamond
Printed and bound by Graphicom in Vicenza, Italy

Front cover: courtesy of Topham Picturepoint
Back cover: courtesy of Mary Evans Picture Library

Contents

Early Life

Mary Seacole was born in Kingston, capital of the British island of Jamaica, in 1805. She did not give us this year herself, nor the precise day or month of her birth. She was shy of divulging such details and, in response to the question in later life, she wrote that *as a female and a widow, I may be well excused giving the precise date of this important event. But I do not mind confessing that the century and myself were both young together and . . . we have grown side by side into age and consequence.*[1]

In the early 19th century, the question of colour was a major issue in Jamaica. Early researchers have commented that in order to fully understand Mary Seacole's achievements, her work must be measured against the time in which she lived and the restrictions under which she had to operate. In 1807, two years after her birth, Britain had abolished the slave trade, but the institution of slavery persisted. In order to enjoy civil rights, in Jamaican society at this time, colour was all important and throughout her childhood and for the rest of her life, Mary would have been aware of its relevance. According to Rex Nettleford, for those aspiring to become citizens, 'the most difficult obligation of all in the scheme of preparation would have been the dilution of colour. It took three generations to become a Jamaican white by law.' Those wishing to gain social ascendancy were careful to choose partners 'to ensure that offsprings would enjoy in the next generation, what Free Coloured or black mothers could not in their own.' Mary Seacole was the child of that class in Jamaica known as the Free Coloureds who 'helped to perpetuate the very basis on which the majority of the population (who were black) were denied that freedom.' Indeed the Free Coloureds of Jamaica were placed in a paradoxical situation at this time, unlike the black slave who had to fight for freedom of expression and allied rights. Although the Free Coloureds could express themselves through the process of free exchange, for example, petitioning, they did so on limited terms. But importantly, they were free people in a slave society and as such the 'distinction had to be made between the slave and free men, despite the fact that one set of free men [whites] made little or no distinction between another set of free men [Free Coloureds] and slaves.' Many Free Coloureds were, like whites, owners of property, including slaves. They believed implicitly in slave-holding and were against abolition. While many petitions were governed by law, some were embodied in customs and conventions. Thus, the hierarchy of colour found expression in both media, 'giving legitimacy to carefully measured drops of white blood that flowed in the veins of Free Coloureds. The acquisition of privileges would *ipso facto* mean the elevation to whiteness which was in any case

Slaves cutting cane, an illustration from *Notes on the Present Conditions of the Negroes in Jamaica* by Henry Thomas de la Beche. 1825

necessary to determine eligibility for rights and privileges – a vicious circle.' Whites used the Free Coloured class as a buffer between themselves and the potentially rebellious Blacks. Nonetheless, this gave most Free Coloureds a sense of purpose despite their disabilities. It was through this system of special privileges that many of the Free Coloureds were able to gain access to some of society's channels of advancement so that they could prove themselves. And by reason of growing wealth, many Free Coloured persons could travel to England and establish connections with articulate and fairly influential persons, including politicians. The trouble with the Free Coloureds of early 19th-century Creole Jamaica, however, was that in their fight for freedom of expression and other civil rights, they failed to commit themselves to a belief in the prudence or necessity of universal privileges for everyone in their society. As a group, at this time of slavery, the Free Coloureds seemed to have lacked anything approaching an independent ideology for freedom. They made the unpardonable error of insisting that they were eligible for freedom because they too were of white blood. Their stand was even more outrageous because the Whites in their midst did not regard them as white and did all they could to ensure that any elevation to that much coveted ethnic status would take no fewer than three generations. 'The Creolization process was itself further distorted by the integration into the very process of the dependency syndrome, the imitative ideal,' as Nettleford put it, 'and the notion that what was white was right and what came from black thought much less so.'[2] Thus Free Coloureds committed an error of judgement by adapting in their quest for freedom, a game of which the rules were set by Whites.

Mary's father was a soldier, a Scotsman. While in Kingston, he stayed in a boarding house run by her mother, a free local woman of mixed black and white parents. She was, according to Jane Robinson, 'probably a mulatto which would make Mary technically a quadroon'.[3]

A mulatto is a person of mixed parentage, one being white, the other black. The term quadroon referred to another mix of parentage, namely one mulatto and one white parent. In Jamaica, people of these groupings were also known as the Free Coloureds.

Mary was always proud of her complexion and, the fairer one was, the greater the advantages, as we shall see later. Mary's mother was an admirable doctress of high repute amongst the officers and soldiers of both the Army and Navy and their wives, who were stationed at Kingston.

In the 1780s, the islands in the West Indies enjoyed an economic boom, during which vast fortunes were made. The chief source of this wealth was sugar, but there were other smaller, but valuable crops like coffee and indigo. No wonder then that in 1789 one-fifth of Britain's foreign trade was with the British West Indies and by the 1790s, it had increased to a third. By the late 1790s, the region was responsible for four-fifths of British overseas capital investments and provided over one-eighth of the government's £31.5 million total net revenue through direct taxes and duties. Not surprisingly, to protect British vested interests, large naval and military forces were deployed to the Caribbean. With so much at stake, Britain took no chances with rivals and with the superior force at its command, new territories were colonised. In such operations, Britain was more successful with the smaller islands than the larger ones. Nonetheless, the sheer scale of Britain's presence and power was impressive. 'Dozens of regiments' served in the West Indies. Between 1793 and 1801, 'some 69 line infantry regiments were sent there. Another 24 followed between 1803 and 1815.'[4]

It was to her father that Mary attributed her *affection for a camp life* and her sympathy for *the pomp, pride and circumstances of glorious war*. She seemed fascinated by war from an early age. It is clear that she was close to her father, a man of the times, a man of action and principle. She was inclined to believe that the Scottish blood in her veins was responsible for her incredibly high level of energy and activity which she said were not always to be found in Creoles. It is this that had impelled her towards a life characterised by variety. To her, the thought of doing one thing for too long was a dismal prospect. The term 'lazy Creole' was a well-known negative reference to Jamaicans (and black people generally) at the time. But this was a stereotype from which she distanced herself. She was different, very much so, and determined to prove her worth. She was unwilling to be tainted by the accusation of indolence. It is significant that early in her life, she was aware of a restless energy within, an impulse which kept her on the move, never idle. It was almost second nature for her to be active. *I have never wanted inclination to rove*, she wrote, *nor will powerful enough to find a way to carry out my wishes*, qualities that had led her to many countries and brought her *into some strange and amusing adventures.*[5]

Mary's mother, a free woman, ran a hotel called Blundell Hall, where British sailors and soldiers who were stationed in the nearby camp, Up-Park, or the military station at Newcastle met, socialised and convalesced. Soon, through keen interest and hard work, Mary's mother gained a well-deserved reputation. Notable among her successes as a competent 'doctress,' was the use of herbal remedies to help the victims of tropical maladies and general sickness.[6] The death rate among British troops due to tropical disease was very high. According to one account, from 1793 to 1802, 'an estimated 45,000 British soldiers died in the West Indies, including about 1,500 officers, nearly all from fevers. In 1796 alone some 41 per cent of the white soldiers died, most of them having arrived within the past year. In the following years, efforts were made to keep white troops out of unhealthy garrisons. As a result, the mortality rate dropped to 15 per cent in 1800 and remained at about 14 per cent from 1803 to 1815. Nevertheless, about 20,000 men died from fevers, including 500 officers.'[7] Mary's mother's herbal remedies proved to be effective treatments. About the time that she was a practitioner of the herbal medical art, Thomas Dancer was convinced of the value of Jamaica local medicine and wrote in his book *The Medical Assistant* that 'many of the Simples of [this] Country are endued with considerable efficacy and may be substituted for the Official ones'.[8] Mary's mother was therefore an important person in Kingston, who attended to the European officers and men at her lodging house. Much earlier, in 1780, herbal medicines were applied to cure Britain's greatest hero of the time, Lord Nelson, of dysentery.[9]

Mary was not her parents' only child. She had a brother Edward and a sister Louisa. Her early life was very interesting and very unusual for a non-white child in colonial Jamaica, especially in the time of slavery. Her mother was very close and attentive to her and naturally Mary followed, in so far as she could, in her mother's footsteps. But in spite of this closeness between mother and daughter, there was another woman with whom she spent a good deal of time during her childhood. According to Mary, she was an old lady who treated her as one of her own grandchildren. Nonetheless, the woman's concern and kindness were *no replacement* for Mary's mother. But even being aware of this, Mary recognised that she was so spoiled by the old lady that were it not for seeing her mother and her patients as often as she did, she thought it very likely that she would have grown up *idle and useless*. Clearly she was highly valued, which boosted her self-esteem. Not surprisingly, Mary was imbued with her sense of self and from about the age of twelve she was spending more time at home with their mother and would assist by doing household duties. Often, she would confide in her mother *the ambition to become a doctress* which took *firm root . . . in my mind*. She admitted to being very young and lacking knowledge, but what little she had was gained by observing her mother attend to a doll. The propensity for children to play-act (and Mary was no exception) led her to relate how readily she imposed her 'childish griefs and blandishments' upon the doll. Quick learner that she was, Mary made *good use* of her *dumb companion and confidante*. Thus, her doll was susceptible to every disease that affected the local people, and her fertile, growing mind imagined medical triumphs that resulted in saving a few *valuable lives*. None of these simulations, however, have been as gratifying as fancying the *glow of health* returning to the doll's face after long and life-threatening illness. As ambition got the better of Mary, she was sufficiently into the habit of empathy and sympathy to extend her practice to *dogs and cats* upon whom she transferred their owners' diseases. In turn, she would administer the likely remedies she deemed suitable for the complaints. In time, her ministrations grew more ambitious and in the absence of human patients, she would play out the patient/nurse roles herself.[10]

An early and tranquil view of Kingston Harbour

The sea was always close by, as Mary grew up. Kingston Harbour was crowded with ships of various shapes and sizes. And, as with being lively and ambitious from an early age, Mary was also smitten by a longing to travel. Her imagination ranged freely as she traced her finger upon an old map moving it along and up from island to island in the Caribbean Sea and then across the Atlantic from Jamaica to England. She was fond of the 'stately ships' in Kingston harbour, many of them bound for England. Soon her improbable, girlish longing was realised, for as she explained *circumstances* enabled her to accompany relatives to England while she was still very young. How young? A recent biography dates this first visit to England to 1822 when Mary was about 19 years old.[11] Once again, it is difficult to tell, but this statement raises interesting questions. For example, who were her 'relatives'? Given that it was unlikely that the people she travelled with were black (non-white), who were her fellow travellers? Were they Jamaicans from among the Free Coloured class? We know that her companions were black or non-white. But it is worth speculating whether a white person was also travelling with them. Slavery was the defining factor in colonial life at this time. Yet Mary mentions little or nothing about it in Jamaica, and from the tone of her writing, in retrospect, she seemed little bothered or affected by that 'peculiar institution.' She was eager, though, to expand on her first impressions of the great metropolis, London. It is significant that she came into contact with street-boys who made fun of her colour. In England this was especially interesting to Mary, who was like an island, a conspicuous minority surrounded by a sea of white/pink people. She became acutely self-conscious. Her skin was different, *only a little brown*, which was nearly white.[12]

In the 1820s, there were many black people in and around Central London, although the black population had dwindled to an estimated 10,000 from 15,000 in the 1780s.[13] Anti-slavery and Parliamentary Reform were key issues in London. Thus far, references to Mary's complexion may have mattered much less than they did when she was surrounded by the white multitudes of London. If it had not happened before, it was here that the memory of her skin colour would burn itself into her consciousness. For now, the street boys reminded her at every turn of this aspect of her presence. But although Mary says little or nothing about the matter, it would be very surprising if she did not encounter people in London who were much darker in complexion than her. Generations of black people had lived there and now the evidence in the form of their descendants was to be seen. Indeed, around this time, the young and soon to be famous black London Chartist, William Cuffay, was playing his part in the Chartist campaign for economic and social justice. Years later, at the time of the delivery of the People's Charter to Parliament, he was charged, convicted and transported to Tasmania, where he spent the rest of his days in a workhouse.[14] So Parliamentary reform, Chartism and anti-slavery were issues that all contributed to a raised awareness of the question of colour and freedom among people who were of a darker hue. On these issues, Mary remained silent, but on the matter of her colour, she would return again some years later: *I am only a little brown*, she wrote, *a few shades duskier than the brunettes whom you all admire so much; but my companion was very dark, and a fair (if I can apply the term to her) subject to their rude wit. She was hot-tempered, poor thing! And as there were no policemen to awe the boys and turn our servants' head in those days, our progress through London streets was sometimes a rather chequered one.*[15]

We do not know where Mary stayed for the year she had spent in England before returning to Kingston. But soon she was on her way back, making her second trip to London. This visit was, for the curious young woman, an eye-opener. But why did she return so quickly and without a companion? What was it that had lured her? She had observed the trading and commercial focus of the metropolis which seemed to have enlivened her already burgeoning business sense learnt from her mother. Of an astute, but caring nature, she quickly recognised opportunities and took them. For her, there were no half-measures: only the maximization of profits counted. She took a large stock of West Indian preserves and pickles with her to be sold in England, having clearly seen the potential market for things West Indian. Consumer demand was overwhelming. There was no mistaking the market for her goods in England, that nation of shopkeepers. Thus, on this second visit, she remained in London for two years.

Her return voyage to Jamaica proved to be more adventurous than she had anticipated. It was a trip which very nearly ended in disaster when fire broke out aboard the *Velusia,* the ship in which she was travelling. Suddenly, the cheerful glow of Christmas Eve merriment had changed to great alarm by Boxing Day. Fortunately, for Mary and her fellow passengers, the fire did not spread and no one was killed. Nonetheless, it was a testing time for all concerned for amidst the turmoil, the panic among the passengers and the forbidding expanse of the high seas, Mary held her nerve. *I did not lose my senses,* she wrote years later, but admitted that during the time when the *contest between fire and water was doubtful*, she was pressed to take heed of her own safety and entered into *an amicable arrangement with the ships' cook, whereby in consideration of two pounds – which I was not however, to pay until the crisis arrived – he agreed to lash me on to a large hen-coop.*[16]

The average non-stop voyage time across the Atlantic was between eight and ten days and eventually on arrival in Kingston harbour Mary was glad to step on dry land once more. But danger had not dampened her interest in travel. Soon her wanderlust amplified and propelled her out of Jamaica once more. After a spell in the Caribbean island of New Providence (where she collected shells which she later sold in Kingston), she also visited Haiti and Cuba, islands to which few non-whites had come as visitors.

Back in Kingston, and now in her early twenties, although Mary was as industrious as ever, she found time to visit and nurse her *old indulgent patroness*, who had been ill. Shortly after she died,

Interior of a house from C R Williams' *A Tour through Jamaica.* 1825

Mary returned to her mother's house, where she made herself useful in a variety of ways, which included learning a great deal more of Creole medical art. It was at this time that a Mr. Seacole appeared on the scene. Was he a dashing heroic soldier? Mary's descriptions seem to imply the opposite. We know that the man who had entered Mary's life was Edwin Horatio Hamilton Seacole, but we know not where they first met. The Englishman's name seems to suggest some possible connection to Lord Horatio Nelson, the great English hero, and his mistress Emma Hamilton. There is not much hard evidence to verify such a link, although attempts have been made.[17] Mary said little or nothing about her bethrothal to Edwin Seacole. She may have been too busy and could well not be the sort to wallow or engage in prolonged courtship. What she did say about this man who had come into her life was that after he had timidly proposed to her, they were married. If their engagement was brief, their honeymoon was perhaps even briefer for soon enough, they had established a store at

Born on 29 September 1758 in Norfolk, Horatio Nelson joined the Royal Navy in 1771, and spent much of his early career serving in the West Indies. In 1780, he took part in an attack on a Spanish fort in Nicaragua, where he fell seriously ill and was nursed back to health in Jamaica thanks to the medical skills of the local Creole women. Nelson went on to become the greatest naval commander in British history, winning great victories at the Battle of the Nile, Copenhagen and finally at Trafalgar on 21 October 1805, where he was killed.

Black River. Since her childhood, and now as a vigorous young woman, she was engaged in a punishing schedule of errands and activities to do with her parents' business and with caring of one sort or another.

Because of her parents' close ties with the Army and doctors, Mary Seacole gained invaluable knowledge and experience which she later combined with the folk medicine learnt from her mother.[18] Now as a wife, nursing loomed ever larger as Mary combined this activity with business. With time, her reputation as a 'doctress' surpassed that of her mother. She was now able to deal effectively with diseases such as cholera, yellow fever, malaria and smallpox that frequently struck down and killed Jamaicans. Then, much too soon, she had to come to terms with losing her ailing husband. After they had established their store at Black River, Mary realised how ill Edwin had become. *Poor man!* she wrote, *he was very delicate and before I undertook the charge of him, several doctors had expressed most unfavourable opinions of his health. I kept him alive by kind nursing and attention as long as I could; but at last he grew so ill that we left Black River.* She returned to her mother's home in Kingston and a few weeks later Edwin died. His passing marked a shift in mood, unlike anything Mary had hitherto experienced. It was a bitter blow, her *first great trouble*, which touched her so deeply that a few years later, she wrote: *For days I never stirred – lost to all that passed around me in a stupor of despair*. But with hindsight, she was able to write: *If you had told me that the time would soon come when I should remember this sorrow calmly, I should not have believed it possible and yet it was so.* And with the accumulation of knowledge and wisdom, in her mature years, she differentiated between her response, as a Creole, to such a moment in life, and non-Creoles. *I do not think that we hot-blooded Creoles sorrow less for showing it so impetuously,* she explained, *but I do think that the sharp edge of our grief wears down sooner than theirs who preserve an outward appearance of calmness, and nurse their woe secretly in their hearts.*[19]

Travels: Business and Nursing

In the wake of her husband's death and her mourning, Mary's dear mother also passed away. She was now alone in the world, battling as best she could. But just when it seemed all was lost, the trying struggles that followed taught her invaluable lessons about the cost of success in life. Later she would reflect upon having *turned a bold front to fortune.* As a widow, life was not only lonely, but also financially difficult. But in spite of setbacks, she never allowed herself to succumb to despair or depression and, as a result, she succeeded in gaining not only a living, but also many comforts besides. But even then, her experience of the world led he to conclude that it was by *no means the hard bad world which some selfish people would have us believe.* Whatever Mary was, it was clear to everyone that she was not selfish.[20]

Her optimism was integral to her warm, caring nature. Among other positive characteristics, she was hearty, strong and plain-spoken. She was enterprising and steady enough, maintaining her composure as her fortunes rose and fell. By her own admission, she never thought only of making money. She believed that we were *born to be happy and that the surest way to be wretched is to prize it* [money] *overmuch.* This tallies, to some extent, with other accounts, one in particular, which tended to over-emphasise her profit-making zeal at the expense of her humanitarian concern. Even if the case against her profiteering was not true, she puts money in its proper perspective thus: *Had I done so, I should have mourned over many a promising speculation proving a failure, over many a pan of preserves or guava jelly burnt in the making; and perhaps lost my mind when the great fire of 1843 which devastated Kingston, burnt down my house. As it was, I very nearly lost my life, for I would not leave my house until every chance of saving it had gone, and it was wrapped in flames. But, of course, I set to work again in a humbler way, and rebuilt my house by degrees and restocked it, succeeding better than before.*[21] At the age of 38, pragmatic and full of common sense might be a good description of Mary Seacole.

Why did she succeed better than before? In part, because the environment was conducive. She knew well the limitations under which she operated, but she exploited the space of being a Free Coloured woman, constantly hustling, seeking opportunities and making the most of them when they arose. Her goodness of heart, caring ways and close observation of her mother and others had, by now, gained for her a reputation as a skillful nurse and doctress, which was tested by visits to her home by invalid British officers and their wives and occasionally a naval or military surgeon. Mary learned a great deal from these educated men as she practised her medical art.

Although Mary had many acquaintances, including friends of her former husband, it seemed there was no romantic liaison, a state of being which was through choice. She was confident enough in her own powers and it was not from necessity that she stayed an unprotected female. If anything, one of the hardest struggles of her life at this time was to resist men who pressed her to marry them. She leaves us in no doubt as to what she felt about marriage at this time. Clearly, she was not preoccupied by this institution. Of greater value to her was the presence of officers of all ranks who were guests in her boarding-house. More and more, her reputation grew and she became well-known among the soldiers who visited Jamaica. The wounded and ailing respected her as a motherly figure. And with her Scottish background, her house was most welcoming, home from home, especially for the British soldiers. Americans were also regular visitors and business, it seemed, ran smoothly.

An etching of Kingston Court House on an election day. 1850

Then in 1850 (when she was 45 years old), Jamaica was struck by cholera. The origin of the outbreak, in Mary's view, were the garments of an infected person who had travelled on a steamer from New Orleans. While the disease spread, one of her lodgers, a doctor, took a keen interest in knowing what treatment was required. Naturally Mary took note. The knowledge she gained was invaluable. That same year, her brother Edward had left Kingston for the Isthmus of Panama, then described as the 'high-road to and from golden California', where he had established a considerable store and hotel. She found his lead irresistible, all the more as visitors came and went leaving her with their exciting stories. An additional reason, it seemed, for her to make the journey to Chagres was her brother's weak constitution. Once the decision was made, she placed her house in the hands of a cousin and made garments such as coats, trousers and shirts, and foodstuffs – preserves, guava jelly and other delicacies, also preserved meats, vegetables and eggs – all of which she felt sure her brother would need. With this baggage, she travelled to

Panama. Thus the urge to roam (her father's influence) was accompanied by the prospect of nursing and selling (her mother's influence) of much-needed foodstuffs.

Her journey across the Isthmus was short. But while it was *insignificant* in distance, it was by no means *an easy one.*[22] On either side of this land mass were the two great oceans, the Atlantic and Pacific. If Mary was in awe of them, she was hardly impressed by life in the Isthmus, where the lack of civilisation struck her powerfully. How unlike colonial Jamaica it was. She was not impressed. Chagres and Panama were appalling places and the California Gold Rush did little to make them more attractive. It was a time when thousands of people were crossing the Isthmus to reach the west coast of the United States. A combination of poverty, disease and lawlessness blighted the area. The more mature Mrs Seacole, the widowed businesswoman was trying to make a living in a dirt town with little or no prospects. Not surprisingly, she moved on. The steamer she travelled in went on to Navy Bay, which was hardly an improvement on the place she had just left. She described it as a luckless, dreary spot, swampland in which the houses were built upon piles. For the health-conscious Mary, this was a dangerous environment. Her concern that it was a nursery for ague, fever and eventually death was echoed by many who had travelled there with her. But this potential for disease did not tempt her to speed ahead to reach her brother. Instead, it was her humanitarian concern, her desire to help others, the victims of disease that had over-run Navy Bay. Although her stay there was short, just one night, it was enough to call her medicine chest into requisition. Sadly, what the sick wanted were remedies which she could not give – warmth, nourishment and fresh air. The scene she beheld was that of men dying from sheer exhaustion.

From here, Mary began her journey to Panama. The first stage was by railway to Gatun, some 12 miles away. En route, she noted that unhealthy stretches of countryside gave way to glimpses of hills in the distance that were reminiscent of the English countryside.[23] The true cost of the railway on which she travelled was, however, thousands of lives. The line ended at Gatun and she travelled on by the river to Chagres, then to Gorgona before finally arriving at Cruces, where her brother lived and worked. Now, as previously, she said little or nothing about her sister Louisa. At this stage, although Mary's self-possession, her independence of mind has become more pronounced, it is important to note that she did not travel alone. She was accompanied by her assistants, a black servant 'Mac' and a little girl. They not only kept her company, but may also have afforded her, as a lone female traveller, much-needed protection in some quite outlandish places. One of the significant lessons of this journey from Jamaica to Cruces was the knowledge that there were 'two species' of individuals whom Mary found to be the same wherever she went – porters and lawyers. Her unsatisfactory dealings with these men were compounded by other problems, such as the loss of several articles from her luggage. The fact that she had hired her

A print of the first excavations for the Panama Canal. 1880

own boat gives a clear indication of her energy, drive and resourcefulness. She could not be fobbed-off easily. If her path was blocked, she would look for another route, which says much for her inventiveness.

In her travels, she was reminded of, and came to learn more about, her colour. Did she have a problem with this? Many years later, she explained herself thus: *I think if I have a little prejudice against our cousins across the Atlantic – and I do confess to a little – it is not unreasonable. I have a few shades of deeper brown upon my skin which shows me related – and I am proud of the relationship – to those poor mortals whom you once held enslaved and whose bodies America still owns. And having this bond and knowing what slavery is; having seen with my eyes and heard with my ears proof positive enough of its horrors – let others affect to doubt them if they will – is it surprising that I should be somewhat impatient of the airs of superiority which many Americans have endeavoured to assume over me?*[24]

With renewed determination, she eventually succeeded in hiring a boat which took her on the last leg to Cruces. Although travel excited her, its wear and tear took its toll. She disembarked tired, wretched and out of temper.

On arrival in Cruces, Mary looked forward to staying at her brother's Independent Hotel, which she hoped could not fail to be acceptable, especially after a long night on the wretched boat. And sure enough, when they met, Edward had the kindest welcome in his face. But, as he led the way to his house, disillusionment was not long in coming. Mary surveyed the street and its surroundings as they walked and was surprised by what she found. *I was miserably unprepared for the reception that awaited me*, she recalled. Amidst the dampness, dirt and confusion, a crowd of gold-diggers had encamped. Stiff, cold and hungry, when she eventually reached her destination, she was disappointed to find that the Independent Hotel was a miserable-looking long, low hut, built of rough, unhewn, unplanned logs filled up with mud. Apart from the lack of space and privacy, she speculated that guests engaging in orgies was not out of the question, and rest, warmth and comfort were miserable delusions. By now, she had run out of patience with her brother. *What am I to do? Why did you ever bring me to this place? See what a state I am in – cold, hungry and wretched. I want to wash, to change my clothes, to eat.*[25]

Mary's questions and complaints were met with a shake of the head and a shrug of the shoulder by Edward. She realised it was a strange life she had come to and, for a while, attributed her troubles to the novelty of her position. But a change here was not as good as a rest. She watched the visitors come and go, especially passengers on their way to and from California. Gold-digging was clearly on their minds, but Mary soon found out that a prized objective of all the travellers was dinner or supper. In addition, wine and spirits were available but according to Mary, the Americans seldom partook.

Gambling, which somehow seemed linked to gold prospecting, was not allowed in Edward's Hotel. There was an expectant feverish excitement among travellers and prospectors, but for travel-weary Mary, rest was uppermost in her mind. She needed a bed, but all rooms were taken. Eventually, as she lay on the floor, tiredness and sleep overtook her. The next morning after breakfast and the departure of guests, passengers and others, Mary left Cruces to its unhealthy solitude.

In her wandering life, it was helpful that Mary was now in Cruces, where she declared that she had never known *what it is to despair or even to despond.* Did this mean that a night's rest had so invigorated her that she could face anything? More accurately perhaps was the fact that she was blessed with an unusually strong physical constitution. Where others were lethargic, she exuded robustness. She recognised and welcomed the 'bright side' of life in the town and became involved in local schemes. Ever ambitious, she aspired to open her own hotel but for now she was prepared to bide her time by putting up at her brother's house. Soon cholera broke out in Cruces and local people laid the blame for the disease on a traveller from New Orleans, a port that seemed to harbour carriers. Predictably, Mary Seacole was ready and willing to help. In fact, she was so prepared that one wonders whether she was expecting it. She was conscious of her surroundings, a keen and astute observer. In later life she explained: *There was no doctor in Cruces; the nearest approach to one was a little timid dentist, who was there by accident and who refused to prescribe for the sufferer, and I was obliged to do my best.* With her medicine kit, which she carried on her travels, she was usually the first on the scene. In Cruces she hurried to the first patient and applied the appropriate remedies. She described this case as *very obstinate* and *by dint of mustard emetics, warm fomentations, mustard plasters on the stomach and the back, and calomel, at first in large then in gradually smaller doses, I succeeded in saving my first cholera patient in Cruces.* The hope of local people that the disease would eventually pass away after a few days was a false one. With frightful suddenness, the cholera spread rapidly and Mary was so fully employed that she scarcely had much rest. But far from complaining, she was surprised by the calamity and her response to it. *I do not deny (it is the only thing indeed that I have to be proud of) that I am pleased and gratified when I look upon my past life to see times when now and then, and places here and there, when and where I have been enabled to benefit my fellow-creatures suffering from ills my skill could often remedy.*[26]

Quick and willing learner that she was, Mary soon realised the power of the disease. There was little fight among those affected, she noted. There was not much resistance. The people's *slavish despair* before the plague is how Mary Seacole later put it. There was not even *the feeblest show of resistance.* Invoking the Saints with *passionate prayers and cries* was not enough. The environment was not conducive to fighting disease. She was not religious, being pragmatic and brutally honest when she wrote: *Very likely the Saints would have got the credit of helping them if they had helped them-selves; but the poor cowards never stirred a finger to clean out their close, reeking huts, or rid the damp street of the rotting accumulation of months.* Very quickly it became clear that the people of Cruces needed her. As she put it, *their chief reliance was on 'the yellow woman from Jamaica with the cholera medicine.'* This did not surprise Mary because *the Spanish doctor . . . was unfamiliar with the terrible disease he was called on to do battle with.*[27]

Mary received adequate pay for her services from those few who were well-off, but she had to be content with thanks from the impoverished majority. Unpleasant a task as it was, she preferred working with the American store and hotel-keeper, rather than the boatmen and muleteers, who suffered terrible losses, in scenes of horror that were unforgettable. As the plague claimed more lives, the demands on Mary's time increased. She had little time to think. Her attention to the sick and dying was total. Then, she was confronted with a major decision. Following the death of a one-year-old child, her powerlessness to save it provoked in her a new approach to dealing with cholera. With the child's lifeless body in her arms, she thought of a novel idea. Put simply, she felt she could learn from the child's death. The time had come to be bold in thought and action. If she could examine the dead child, she thought, she could learn a great deal about the disease which showed no sign of dying out. The situation was desperate; there was no time to lose. Her mind was made up. She felt justified in taking the step she had intended: *I knew the fled spirit would not reproach me, for I had done all I could for it in life – had shed tears over it, and prayed for it.* Now on a cold grey morning, as the child was taken away for burial, Mary followed the man who carried the body. She bribed the man to take a lonely path that led to the riverside. They both stopped at a bushy part of the river bank and

Mary persuaded the man to assist her in performing her first and last post-mortem examination. It was, to say the least, a courageous act, an extraordinary initiative on Mary's part and the results were *decidedly useful*, she recalled in later years. Though medical men were already familiar with the kind of thing that she had done in secrecy, the knowledge she had gained bolstered her confidence as a nurse and 'Doctress'.[28]

After burying the child, Mary and her accomplice slipped back into Cruces like guilty things. But the silver experiment yielded a golden pay-off, for the knowledge she had gained was invaluable to her. She applied herself to her practice and was now more confident that she knew which medicines worked and which did not. She confirmed this, some years later when she wrote that *the simplest remedies* were perhaps the best. *Mustard plasters and emetics and calomel; the mercury applied externally, where the veins were nearest the surface, were my usual resources.* She dreaded opium and to the thirsty patient, she gave water *in which cinnamon had been boiled. Above all, I never neglected to apply mustard poultices to the stomach, spine and neck and particularly to keep my patient warm about the region of the heart.* Qualified medical doctors may have treated these patients differently, but persistent care after the disease had passed was Mary's approach. What did she learn from all this? The *great conclusion* which her practice among cholera sufferers had brought her to was *the old one that few constitutions permitted the use of exactly similar remedies and that the course of treatment which saved one man, would, if persisted in have very likely killed his brother.* Throughout the epidemic, her presence was required here, there and everywhere. She willingly sacrificed herself to the care of others and in so doing, she was exposed to the disease. Then, one day, she realised her own vulnerability when symptoms of cholera showed themselves in her. Not knowing whom she should turn to, she hurried to her brother's house, where she experienced a frightening moment, when an unpleasant chill overtook her and she was forced to go to bed. Other symptoms followed and before night-fall, she had become a victim of the dreaded cholera, which had attacked *perhaps its greatest foe in Cruces.*[29]

This was a cruel blow for Mary. News that she was afflicted spread fast. And when the people of Cruces heard, they were magnanimous in showing their gratitude, concern and sympathy for the 'Yellow Doctress.' While she was grateful, the attention that she received had its down side. Being ill was, for Mary, a rare experience, which deepened her understanding. As she later reflected: *Indeed when I most wanted quiet, it was difficult to keep out the sympathising Americans and sorrowing natives who came to inquire after me; and who, not content with making their inquiries, and leaving their offerings of blankets, flannel etc, must see with their own eyes what chance the yellow woman had of recovery. The rickety door of my little room could never be kept shut for many minutes together. A visitor would open it silently, poke his long face in with an expression of sympathy that almost made me laugh in spite of my pain, draw it out again, between the narrowest possible opening, as if he were anxious to admit as little air as he could; while another would come in boldly and after looking at me curiously and ignorantly as he would eye a horse or nigger, he had some thoughts of making a bid for, would help to carpet my room, with the result perhaps of his meditations and saying gravely, give place to another and another yet, until I almost inclined to throw something at them and call them bad names, like the Scots King does the ghosts in the play.*

Fortunately, Mary had only a mild attack of cholera, though for a while she felt *weak and exhausted.* It was the local population's good fortune that a few weeks later, there were no more new cases of the disease and it eventually stopped. Thereafter, the survivors of Cruces pursued life with characteristic briskness and selfishness, as the horrors of the cholera faded. With her reputation enhanced, there was much in store for Mary Seacole. The Americans who ran the place retained her services as their 'medical attendant.' While this post kept her as busy as possible, it did not deflect her attention from pursuing her original purpose of running a hotel in Cruces. Both her medical work and ambition as hotelier seemed to bring balance in her life which she welcomed. This quest for centredness, for balance will recur time and again in Mary's life. At last, she found a building which she hoped to transform into her hotel. Now economic considerations preoccupied her. Though the rent of £20 a month was *reasonable*, there was room for improvement. Eventually, the building which she regarded as a rude hut was refurbished with a variety of material, including calico of bright colours, with fringes, frills and bows, which gave much pleasure to the Americans. She was determined to keep lodgers out, running the place solely as an eating-house. Her staff included Mac (her black servant), a little girl and a local cook. Whatever she did learn from her brother about the hotel business, ultimately, the head-strong Mary fixed her own charges and explained that *for an ordinary dinner my charge was four shillings; eggs and chickens were...distant luxuries and fetched high prices.*[30]

In those early days, Mary described the majority of her clients on their way to California, as rough, rude, dirty and quarrelsome. But she regarded those few who were more civilised as being more dangerous. It was therefore no surprise that before long, she grew very tired of life in Cruces, even though she made money quickly. But thoughts of leaving also moved her to press her brother to return to Kingston. While managing her hotel in Cruces, Mary realised once more how unprotected a female she was. At times, she was faced with the difficult task of managing rowdy travellers and guests. The coarse females and the dinner habits of many Americans were of special interest to Mary, who observed that: *Very often quarrels would arise during the progress of dinner; and more than once I thought the knives which they nearly swallowed at every mouthful, would have been turned against one another. It was, I always thought, extremely fortunate that the reckless men rarely stimulated their excitable passions with strong drink. Tea and coffee were the common beverages of the Americans; Englishmen and men of other nations, being generally distinguishable by their demand for wine and spirits. But the Yankee's capacity for swilling tea and coffee was prodigious! I saw one man drink 10 cups of coffee; and finding his appetite still unsatisfied, I ran across to my brother for advice. There was a merry twinkle in his eyes as he whispered 'I always put in a good spoonful of salt after the 6th cup. It chokes them off admirably.'*[31]

Theft and cheating was endemic among unscrupulous travellers. And once again, it was only the 'cutest yankee' who could outwit the vigilant Mary. She learned fast about the business as the challenges confronted her. Gambling, for example, while being a business that accrued the primary reward of money made from the gold-seekers, no one cared enough to make gambling attractive. Occasionally, however, a few 'distinguished' travellers passed her way. One of them, Mary says in her autobiography, was Lola Montez, who was bound for California; another was Catherine Hayes, the singer. But this reference to Montez is problematic, for as one writer states, Lola was never in Cruces.[32]

The problem that confronted Mary was that the majority of the crowds were very rowdy. They tended to devalue life, ready on a whim to kill or be killed over the slightest provocation. The intimidating nature of a crowd's arrival or departure

The infamous dancer and 'adventuress' Lola Montez was born Elizabeth Rosanna Gilbert on 17 February 1821 in Ireland. She trained as a dancer in Spain where she adopted her stage name. Her career in England collapsed when it was revealed she was not actually a 'Spanish dancer,' but she moved to the Continent, where in 1846 she became involved with the 60-year-old King Ludwig I of Bavaria, who made her a countess, but two years later popular hostility forced her to leave the country. After travelling the world dancing and later lecturing, she died in New York on 17 January 1861.

always contained potentially violent elements. The noise they made was loud. Their behaviour was raucous. But even this could not deflect Mary's attention away from an aspect of life there that commanded her attention. She wrote: *Against the Negroes, of whom there were many in the Isthmus, and who almost invariably filled the municipal offices, and took the lead in every way, the Yankees had a strong prejudice; but it was wonderful to see how freedom and equality elevate man, and the same Negro who perhaps in Tennessee would have cowered like a beaten child or dog beneath an American's uplifted hand, would face him boldly here, and by equal courage and superior physical strength cow his old oppressor.*[33]

By now, Mary had come to know the local community well enough to treat elements of it with due caution. Time and again, certain themes emerge: crime and punishment, law and order. Thieving was prevalent, but Mary was careful to exclude the 'Negroes' (African-Americans) from this practised and skilful activity. An honest day's work for an honest day's pay could not be applied there, even though punishment was quite severe. In this lawless place, Mary's approach to justice was simple: she did not rely on the law for protection, for ultimately it was an expensive luxury. She cited Americans as being the group that was hardest to bring to justice. Put simply, some got away with murder.

It was at the end of the rainy season that Mary prepared to leave Cruces for Gorgona. But before doing so, it was customary for store and hotel-keepers to exchange visits and attended each other's parties. Mary's popularity in the community had grown, partly because of her medical contribution during the cholera. Of the many invitations which she received the most important was held on American Independence Day at her brother's Hotel, where high-spirited Americans dined. Much champagne was drunk and after patriotic toasts, attention was focused on Mary whose keen ear picked up what was said at the time! The speaker was a *thin, sallow-looking* American who spoke rapidly. He said: *'Well, gentlemen, I expect you'll all support me in a drinking of this toast that I du -----. Aunty Seacole, gentlemen; I give you, Aunty Seacole -----. We can't du less for her, after what she's done for us -----, when the cholera was among us, gentlemen -----, not many months ago -----. So, I say, God bless the best yaller woman He ever made -----, from Jamaica, gentlemen -----, from the Isle of Springs. Well, gentlemen, I expect there are only tu things we're vexed for; and the first is, that she ain't one of us, a citizen of the great United States -----; and the other thing is, gentlemen -----, that Providence made her a yaller woman. I calculate, gentlemen, you're all as vexed as I am that she's not wholly white, but I du reckon on your rejoicing with me that she's so many shades removed from being entirely black! -----; and I guess, if we could bleach her by any means we would -----, and thus make her as acceptable in any company as she deserves to be. Gentlemen, I give you Aunty Seacole!'*

The speaker was applauded, but Mary was not amused. Incensed by the reference to her colour, although her brother cautioned her not to speak too freely, she said: *'Gentlemen — I return you my best thanks for your kindness in drinking my health. As for what I have done in Cruces, Providence evidently made me to be useful, and I can't help it. But I must say that I don't altogether appreciate your friend's kind wishes with respect to my complexion. If it had been as dark as any nigger's I should have been just as happy and as useful, and as much respected by those whose respect I value; and as to his offer of bleaching me. I should, even if it were practicable, decline it without any thanks. As to the society which the process might gain me admission into, all I can say is that, judging from the specimens I have met with here and elsewhere, I don't think that I shall lose much by being excluded from it. So, gentlemen, I drink to you and the general reformation of American manners.'* The sense of herself and how others viewed her aroused strong responses from Mary. She did not think her speech was well-received, believing that although the Americans laughed *good naturedly*, it was because she was *a somewhat privileged person*.[34] This hypocrisy was not to her liking for she would have much preferred it if they had been angry.

With her mind set on moving on to Gorgona, although business was very much on her mind, she was concerned about her brother who was young and prone to illness. In Gorgona, Mary's business as an hotelier was uppermost in her mind. When, at last, she found a miserable little hut for sale and bought it for $100, she set about renovating it. The accommodation here was, in some respects, superior to her previous property. Here, she was willing to try something different. She decided to provide the public, her customers with an unusual, an almost exclusive service. Her establishment would be open, in large part, to entertain 'ladies' and those in need of care and attention. In the meantime, she persisted in trying to influence her brother. But in spite of her best efforts to persuade him to leave the Isthmus of Panama, she began to have serious thoughts about leaving him there.

Also at this time, there were gaps in Mary's life, which she felt needed to be filled. The limitations were obvious, she thought. She needed to explore, to move on. But she was careful to state that it was not *altogether my old roving inclination which led me to desire a change*. She did not think that her life as it was being lived was *agreeable for a woman with the least delicacy or refinement; and of female society I had none*. But having said this, she was prone to avoid the women that came her way. She found many of them to be either bad or disagreeable and she had special difficulty dealing with most women from the southern states of America, because *they showed an instinctive repugnance against any one whose countenance claimed for her kindred with their slaves, my position was far from a pleasant one . . . They were glad of my stores and comforts, I made money out of their wants; nor do I think our*

SECOND HOTEL   29

bond of connection was ever close. But if this caused her no annoyance, she leaves us in no doubt of her magnanimity when she states that *if any of them came to me sick and suffering (I say this out of simple justice to myself) I forget everything, except that she was my sister and that it was my duty to help her.*[35]

In Gorgona, as in Cruces, Mary reflected, the likelihood of flooding was real and although her hotel was on higher ground, nonetheless, she was known to have suffered *some distressing losses*. Then, when fire ravaged Gorgona, Mary had had enough. Leaving her hotel in her brother's hands, she prepared to return to Kingston.

But leaving the calamities of this place to return home was not the end of her discomfiture or distress, for a hitherto new experience awaited her at the Navy Bay quayside. She was anxious to get home and had booked her passage on the first steamer, which was American-owned. Late in the evening of her departure, she bade farewell to friends with whom she had been staying and boarded the steamer. One of her very kind friends, an American merchant approached her with the advice that she should 'delay' her journey until an English steamer was available. This struck Mary as being odd, all the more because the American friend could not give a good reason for delaying her trip. And so without further delay Mary proceeded with Mac and her little maid to pass through a crowd of female passengers on her way to the saloon. After a short while, two women came up and questioned her.

'*Where air you going?*'
'*To Kingston.*'
'*And how air you going?*'
'*By sea.*'
'*Don't be impertinent yaller woman. By what conveyance are you going?*'
'*By steamer of course. I've paid for my passage.*'

Mary kept calm as the women went away in the full knowledge

that she had paid for her passage. This was the end of the matter as far as she was concerned. But soon she was surrounded by eight or nine white women who repeated the questions about her destination and how she was going to get there. Mary's answers raised quite a storm of uncomplimentary remarks.

'Guess a nigger woman don't go along with us in this saloon,' said one. 'I never travelled with a nigger yet, and I expect I shan't begin now,' said another; while some children had taken my little servant Mary in hand, and were practising on her the politenesses which their parents were favouring me with – only, as is the wont of children, they were crueller. I cannot help it if I shock my readers; but the truth is, that one positively spat in poor little Mary's frightened yellow face.

At last an old American lady came to where I sat and gave me some staid advice. 'Well, now, I tell you for your good, you'd better quit this, and not drive my people to extremities. If you do, you'll be sorry for it, I expect.' Thus harassed, I appealed to the stewardess – a tall sour-looking woman, flat and thin as a dressed-up broomstick. She asked me sundry questions as to how and when I had taken my passage; until, tired beyond all endurance, I said, 'My good woman, put me anywhere – under the boat – in your store-room, so that I can get to Kingston somehow.' But the stewardess was not to be moved.'

'There's nowhere but the saloon and you can't expect to stay with the white people, that's clear. Flesh and blood can stand a good deal of aggravation; but not that! If the Britishers is so took up with coloured people, that's their business; but it won't do here!'

This last remark was in answer to an Englishman whose advice to me was not to leave my seat for any of them. He made matters worse; until at last I lost my temper, and calling Mac, made him get my things together, and went up to the Captain – a good honest man. He and some of the black crew and the black cook, who showed his teeth most viciously, were much annoyed. Muttering about its being a custom of the country, the Captain gave me an order upon the agent for the money

I had paid; and so, at twelve o'clock at night, I was landed again upon the wharf of Navy Bay! My American friends were vastly annoyed, but not much surprised; and two days later, the English steamer, the Eagle in charge of my old friend Capt B-----, touched Navy Bay and carried me to Kingston.[36]

Determined to Serve

In 1853, on her return to Jamaica from Panama, Mary found her services were needed because of an outbreak of yellow fever which had hit the island with such severity that she thought it would destroy the English people on the island. The raging epidemic claimed the lives of many, including some who were close to Mary. In Mary's house, there were many sufferers — officers, wives and children. Fortunately for these victims, Mary was in the right

A nineteenth century lithograph of a Jamaican landscape

place at the right time. But although she had seen a great deal of suffering and death, she found these Jamaican scenes more diffi-cult to bear than any at which she had previously been present. In the circumstances, she found that apart from trying to lift the spirits of the patient, she also had the difficult task of helping the bereaved. *It was a terrible thing to see young people in the youth and bloom of life suddenly stricken down,* she wrote, *not in battle with an enemy that threatened their country, but in vain contest with a climate that refused to adopt them. Indeed, the mother country pays a dear price for the possession of her colonies.* Her empathy and sympathy for England and Britishness was not in doubt. Although she would later generalise, it is clear she was referring to herself when she wrote: *I think all who were familiar with the West Indies will acknowledge that Nature has been favourable to strangers in a few respects and that one of these had been instilling into the hearts of the Creoles an affection for English people and an anxiety for their welfare, which shows itself warmest when they are sick and suffering.* Furthermore, she pointed to another benefit that had been conferred upon the English, namely the practice among Creoles of the healing art, which induced them *to seek out the simple remedies which are available for the terrible diseases by which foreigners are attacked, and which are found growing under the same circumstances which produce the ills they minister to. So true is it that beside the nettle ever grows the cure for its sting.* Thus far, it had been difficult for Mary Seacole to avoid human suffering, dying and death. For better or worse, these were the scenes with which she was most familiar. Amidst it all, she was not squeamish, but rather forthright in her views on those whom she had *now and then accompanied a little distance on their way into the valley of the shadow of death.* After many years of caring, she expressed her thoughts on death, a fear of which she said no one need be ashamed. *How we bear it depends much upon our constitutions,* she believed. As the number of casualties mounted, she considered the brave men who endured the cruellest amputation with a smile, men who died trembling like children and those who drew their last breath like heroes. But, she declared, she would not trace the peace and resignation she had seen to temperament alone. She was not overly religious, and she expressed her belief thus: *I have stood by receiving the last blessings of Christians; and closing the eyes of those who had nothing to trust but the mercy of a God who will be far more merciful to us than we are to one another; and I say decidedly that the Christian death is the glorious one, as is his life! . . . as the work of the labour of a lifetime make the repose of heaven acceptable.* Nonetheless, proximity to death did not make her insensitive to it. In fact, the smell of death was never far away and the passing of some were more memorable than others. She remembered the death of a man which touched her deeply. His dying moments taught her that when her time comes, she would approach it with a brave, smiling face. This man's demise was the best example of the nobility of dying and in some detail, Mary tells us why. She said she could not divulge the man's name because his friends were still alive. She identified him as a young surgeon, who had been kind to her in many ways, and when he fell ill he was taken to her house. As she nursed him, she grew fond of him, so much so that she felt almost as close to him as his mother who was thousands of miles away in England. The scenes she witnessed were poignant. When the man knew that he would not survive his illness, that death was imminent, he projected a selfless quality which touched Mary. He showed little regard for himself. All his pity, she said, was for those he was leaving behind. Instead of leaving the matter to rest, many years later, in her autobiography, the scene is dramatised further: *It was trying to see his poor hands trembling penning the last few words of leave-taking – trying to see how piteously the poor worn heart longed to see once more the old familiar faces of the loved ones in unconscious happiness at home.* Mary Seacole's feelings were abundant and she felt they were well received. In the absence of the man's loved ones, she was conscious of her supportive role and felt her nursing was worthwhile. *I think he had some fondness for me, or perhaps, his kind heart feigned a feeling that he saw would give me joy; for I used to call him 'my son – my dear child' and weep over him in a very weak and silly manner.* But death, as she reflected, was not to be feared, nor was its effect silly. She then described the young man's final moments of life thus: *He sent for an old friend . . . and when he came, I had to listen to the dictation of his simple will – his dog to one friend, his ring to another, his books to a third, his love and kind wishes to all.* Once this was done, she wrote of her *poor son* as he *prepared himself to die – a child in all save a man's calm courage. He beckons me to raise him in the bed, and as I passed my arms around him, he saw the tears I could not repress rolling down my brown cheeks and thanked me with a few words. 'Let me lay my head upon your breast,' and so he rested, now and then speaking slowly to himself, 'It's only that I miss my mother, but heaven's will be done.' He repeated this many times, until the Heaven beyond sent him in its mercy forgetfulness and his thoughts no longer wandered to his earthly home. I heard glad words feebly uttered as I bent over him – words about 'Heaven – rest – rest.' as I bent over him – a holy Name many times repeated and then with a smile and a stronger voice, 'Home! Home.' And so in a little while my arms no longer held him.*[37] And so the beloved Englishman in Mary's care passed away. As a memento she kept a little gold brooch with a lock of his hair in it. This was sent to her by the dead man's mother as a keepsake in appreciation of Mary's kindness to her son.

In this long drawn-out example of a death-bed scene, we get a sense of how close Mary Seacole had already become to the English, Scottish and Irish soldiers to whom she attended in Jamaica. If anything, the death of the young man had a positive effect on her. She began to see the work before her more clearly. There was a more expansive, greater role for her to play. Thus, when she was called upon by the medical authorities to assist in the recruitment of nurses to be employed at Up-Park Camp, a short distance from Kingston, the dutiful Mary left a few nurses at home and went to do her best to *mitigate the severity of the epidemic.*[38] This was a bold and courageous step.

Nonetheless, some months later, she felt the urge to be on the move again. Her 'rootlessness', it seemed, took hold and she returned to Gorgona to wind up her affairs relating to the hotel she had left behind. She found things had changed little there. At that time she also took the opportunity to visit Panama with her brother, finding it an old-fashioned place with stone houses, almost all of which had been taken over by traders as stores. She then opened a store in Navy Bay, which she ran for the next three months. Here too she found that things were not much different. If anything, the place was even more lawless, characterised by ongoing quarrels, violence and bloodshed. There was no peace to be found and here again, we see Mary Seacole the opportunist, ready to take the next chance. Indeed when an opportunity did present itself at Escribanos, one of the New Granada Gold Mining Company stations some 70 miles from Navy Bay, Mary took it. Legend had it that there were ancient treasures at various remote sites near the village. But getting there was a time-consuming business which Mary could ill-afford, and even when she got there, *the yield of gold*, as she put it, *did not repay the labour and capital necessary to extract it from the quartz.*[39]

Always observant and ready to learn, she was fascinated by the Alcalde of Escribanos, Carlo Alexander. She approved of his handling of the gold mania. The mine belonged to him and she identified him clearly as a 'black man' who was fond of talking of his early life in slavery and how he had escaped enslavement. The superintendent of this mine was Mr. Day, whose invitation had led to Mary being in Escribanos. She tells us that he was a distant cousin of her deceased husband. Mr Day treated her kindly and having been the Alcalde's guest, in the twelve weeks she was there, she had grown to appreciate the new experience to the extent that for a while she was caught up with prospecting for gold. More and more, at this time, she was guided by the experience she gained. She learned fast as her powers of observation developed. Some years later, she recalled these last days of her travels in Central America. With remarkable clarity, she noted: *The foreigners were just as troublesome in this little out of the way place as they were in every other part of Central America; and quarrels were as frequent in our little community as at Cruces or Navy Bay.*[40]

Before she had left Jamaica for Escribanos, it is more than likely that she would have read the news of the 'war in the East,' which related to tensions and conflict between Russia and Turkey. By the early spring of 1854, while she was still in Kingston, British soldiers stationed there would have read and spoken about reports in *The Times* newspaper, which circulated among them. One of these accounts in *The Times* related the brutal Russian attacks which resulted in the death of thousands of Turks. 'The manner in which these attacks have been conducted,' it stated, 'and the tone in which these victories have been celebrated, is sufficient proof that [Russia] will not easily desist from this war and, though we regret none of the protracted efforts which have been made to avert so great an evil, we are not the less prepared to meet it in the last resort by a vigorous resistance.'[41] In the face of this aggression, the British and French governments, the report added, were called upon to make a prompt decision. Consequently, Britain and France joined Turkey in the Crimean War.

The British army had not fought a major European war since 1815, and the administrative problems of mobilising a large body of men were daunting. The armed forces were ill-equipped and bureaucratic incompetence created chaotic scenes at the front, namely a lack of proper clothes, food, tents, medicines and medical attention. The camps soon became a breeding ground for disease, which was compounded by mismanagement and neglect. The rising number of deaths due to disease, far in excess of those who died in combat, aroused growing public interest in Britain. The stark accounts from the war zone by William Howard Russell, the *Times* war correspondent, led to a public outcry, an upsurge of public sympathy and the creation of the Crimean Fund.[42]

Mary Seacole's upbringing, her ups and downs, her travels and her general experience in Jamaica and central America were invaluable, an experience which prepared her physically and mentally and spiritually for future undertakings, for more ambitious travels and work that had already entered her lively mind. If the West Indies was a far outpost of the British Empire, developments in the Crimea promised a greater, even more central theatre of operations, which would be admirably suited to Mary Seacole's opportunistic designs as she left Escribanos and embarked on her journey to England.

A portrait of Mary Seacole before the Crimean War

It may come as a surprise to some readers to learn how eager Mary was to witness the Crimean conflict. Her longing to see and experience war sounds naïve and extraordinary to us today, especially because she was such a caring person. But, she wrote *when I was told that many of the Regiments I had known so well in Jamaica had left England for the scene of action, the desire to join them became stronger than ever.* From then on, she was propelled forward as if by an obsession and soon found herself standing for long periods in deep thought, as she scanned a map of the world. Her eager eyes looked for the place called the Crimea. And there it was, marked by a red cross. She traced the route from Britain to the Crimea, and her growing preoccupation with the difficulties of getting there would vanish. As thoughts of how to get to that place on the map persisted, she had several conversations with friends, mulling over in her mind, *the best scheme I could devise seemed so wild and improbable that I was fain to resign my hopes for a time.*[43]

And so, some 3,000 miles away from England, she first concentrated on making the journey to England from Navy Bay, before considering any further steps. Eventually, the long voyage began and in the autumn of 1854 Mary arrived in London where she closely monitored news from the Crimea. The battle of the Alma had already been fought. She thought of her 'old friends' who were, at the time, just outside Sebastopol. Above all else, she struggled with finding a solution to the problem of how to join them there. But as such thoughts overwhelmed her, she had the presence of mind enough to step back a little and appraise what else was passing through her mind. In London she reflected that, like others, she too was caught up in speculation on gold mines, so feasible in New Granada at the time, but viewing it now from her London perspective it seemed wild and improbable. This was far easier than her growing concern over an unknown battleground. But with the passage of time, her desire had grown so much that she felt compelled to be of service. The prospect of joining 'old friends' of the 97th and 48th and other regiments fighting enemies that were worse than yellow fever or cholera. This last statement about the Russians was not to infer that they were to be compared with diseases and therefore less than men. On the contrary, men were men, but thoughts of her compatriots so overwhelmed her that speculation in gold gave way to devoting all her energy to her new scheme.

She was realistic about it and admitted: *Heaven knows it was visionary enough.* For one thing, she was a stranger, entirely unknown amidst the bustle of the teeming millions of the metropolis. She was overwhelmed by the experience of being in London again. Here, in the heart of the British Empire her flagging spirits were bolstered. This was the most extraordinary place she had ever visited, but she had no friends who could help in her venture, and she lamented: *Who would understand why I desired to go and what I desired to do when I got there?* Even with careful accounting, making the near 3,000-mile trip seemed far fetched. She could not be anything less than realistic. She worried that friends would not support her for long. There was also the problem of convincing the British public that *an unknown Creole woman would be useful to their Army before Sebastopol.* And once again, she thought of this as *too improbable an achievement to be thought of for an instant.* She continued to wrestle with the idea and, as it was, sheer persistence and circumstances led her on. Amidst the London winter, she pondered the grim news from the war zone. Now she learned from various quarters of mismanagement, want and suffering among the British forces in the Crimea, and after the battles of Balaclava and Inkerman and the fearful storm of 14 November 1854, in which large quantities of supplies were lost when 16 ships were sunk in Balaclava harbour, her worst fears were realised. It had became increasingly clear that the need for help was urgent, that *the hospitals were full to suffocation, that scarcity and exposure were the fate of all in the camp.* Such news intensified her patriotic feelings, compounded by further depressing reports of hundreds who were wounded and dying at the Scutari hospital, where the medical facilities were woefully inadequate to provide shelter, and the few staff unable to cope with the regular flow of shiploads of casualties sent to them across the storm-tossed Black Sea. With each day, it seemed, the news that reached London was less and less encouraging and by now Mary Seacole was utterly convinced of the dire need in the Crimea. So too were the people of England who, as Mary later reflected, *set about repairing past neglect*. Furthermore, she tried to capture something of the national spirit that was engendered. *In every household busy fingers were working for the poor soldier money flowed in golden streams wherever need was and Christian ladies, mindful of the sublime example, 'I was sick and ye visited me' hastened to volunteer their services by those sick beds which only women know how to soothe and bless.*[44]

Mary felt at one with England's women, but what set her apart was that she harboured a greater desire to be in 'active sympathy' with the British soldiers at war. Although she was an outsider, she was not ashamed to confess sharing in the 'general enthusiasm' which strengthened her longing to be *where the sword or bullet had been busiest and pestilence most rife*. Her confidence was boosted by her background and experience. With hindsight, she would record: *I had seen much of sorrow and death elsewhere, but they had never daunted me; and if I could feel happy binding up the wounds of quarrelsome Americans and treacherous Spaniards, what delight should I not experience if I could be useful to my own 'sons' suffering for a cause it was so glorious to fight for!* Now, all doubts about reaching the scene of action had disappeared. She was positive, focused, and determined to achieve her goal. Her mind was made up *that if the Army wanted nurses, they would be glad of me, and with all the ardour of my nature, which carried me where inclination prompted, I declared that I would go to the Crimea*. More and more, she was driven each day to do something, as the Crimea beckoned. Writing a few years later, she reflected upon her decision: *I should have given up the scheme a score of times in as many days; so regularly did each successive day give birth to a fresh set of rebuffs and disappointments.*[45] As it was, little did she know that the Crimea and her Crimean exploits would become the single most comprehensive, detailed record that we have about her.

What were these disappointments? Mary felt she was well qualified for the work to be done, and as she mulled over the prospects. Feeling that she would be the right woman in the right place, her confidence was high. It was this sense of herself (and a certain degree of audacity) that moved her to present herself at the War Office to serve as a hospital nurse. She was all the more encouraged because she had already dealt with diseases such as cholera, diarrhoea and dysentery that were rife in the Crimea. In the strict professional sense, the accusation of presumption on her part would be inappropriate. She was in no doubt that her services as a nurse would be complementary to the efforts of the over-worked doctors, and, there were many who would testify to her knowledge and experience.

If the application which she made at the War Office was an example of her tenacity, it proved to be a waste of time. Nonetheless, the appearance of this extraordinary 50-year-old un-English woman was so unusual that it caused a good deal of awkwardness among War Office officials. Years later, she wrote: *I have reason to believe that I considerably interfered with the repose of sundry managers and disturbed to an alarming degree, the official gravity of some nice gentlemanly young fellows, who were working out their salaries in an easy, off-hand way.*[46] Thus she had failed in her 'ridiculous' attempt to get an interview with the Secretary of War, but undeterred she approached the Quartermaster-General's department. Here too, she was met with much 'polite enjoyment' and amusement by the gentlemen she spoke to who, in turn, referred her to the Medical Department. This too was worth a try. But alas, she grew tired of the rebuffs.. The experienced nurse and doctress was clearly hurt by these consecutive disappointments. How much more could she, would she take? Three years later, she wrote that *not for a single instant* [was she] *going to blame the authorities who would not listen to the offer of a motherly yellow woman to go to the Crimea and nurse her 'sons'*, since the officials in the War Office knew nothing of her experience and knowledge gained in the West Indies, despite the references she had. She was however unhappy with the official attitude towards her and with hindsight she later expressed her reservations. While war was clearly a serious matter, nonetheless, she wrote that *sometimes very humble actors are of great use in it and if the Reader when he comes to peruse the evidence of those who had to do with the Sebastopol drama, of my share in it, will turn back to this chapter, he will confess perhaps that after all, the impulse which led to the War Department was not unnatural.*[47]

Each time she was stopped, she resorted to other plans. Now her attention was shifted to a new scheme (a plan), which she confessed was *worse devised than the one which had failed*, was to enlist with the nurses who were to go out to the Crimea to join Florence Nightingale. The desire to be with her 'sons' had not diminished one iota. If anything, it increased. Though establishment figures may have perceived it to be so, Mary Seacole never saw her gender as a problem. Being non-white and from one of the oldest and largest of the former slave colonies in the West Indies were also barriers set up against women from the Empire. Overall, women, including Europeans, had to fight for their rights. But as Mary was gradually finding out, she had other disadvantages, even though she was well-qualified for a nursing job. *Feeling that I was one of the very women they most wanted, experienced and fond of the work, I jumped at once to the conclusion that they would gladly enrol me in their number.* But although she waited patiently to be given the Secretary at War's consent to enlist, she had to abandon that hope after being told that *the full complement of nurses had already been secured, and that my offer could not be entertained.* This was the stock answer to those candidates who were regarded as unsuitable. Thus, Mary was turned down for a nursing post. Her determination undimmed, and shored up by patriotism, she decided to try once more. This time she sought an interview with one of Miss Nightingale's colleagues, a woman who proved to be no less obstructive. *I read in her face,* Mary wrote, *the fact that had there been a vacancy, I should not have been chosen to fill it.*[48]

In spite of these rejections, as a last resort, Mary turned to the managers of the Crimean Fund to see if they would assist her by paying her passage to the Crimea. She hoped that there would be work for her to do. But this attempt also failed. It was one more disappointment, but perhaps it was one too many and it took its toll. She now had to face facts and did so in the cold twilight of one winter's evening. Although she did not admit it at the time, the cumulative effect of these negative responses was so great that it was still strong when years later she reflected *upon the ruins of the unselfishness of the motives which induced me to leave England – so certain of service I could render among the sick soldiery, and yet I found it so difficult in my heart for the first and last time, thank Heaven. Was it possible that American prejudices against colour had some root here. Did these ladies shrink from accepting my aid because my blood flowed beneath a somewhat duskier skin than theirs?* she questioned. The predicament she was in drove her to tears. The London streets were bleak and empty, the cold weather keeping the crowds away. She was grief-stricken because of doubt in the minds of the authorities. How could they deny her? The questions she posed deepened her unhappiness so much so that she began to pray out loud in public, attracting strange looks from passers-by. But however odd her behaviour might have seemed to those who saw her at the time, she felt justified in explaining it essentially to her English readers many years later: *I am one of an impulsive people,* she wrote, *and find it hard to put that restraint upon my feelings, which to you is so easy and natural*. After this natural release of pent-up emotion, arising from consecutive disappointments, Mary felt refreshed the next day. She felt relieved, ready to face all comers. She was filled with renewed hope and determination to go to the Crimea, but the problem remained: How would she go? This was now the central question and, all things considered, she answered it forthrightly. The question of money was paramount, especially because she could now see no other way of getting there except at her own expense. This was the bottom line. Then her thoughts turned to those whom she had helped in the past, both patients and doctors. Many of them were now in the Crimea. This was the only way forward, she reasoned: *If the authorities had allowed me, I would willingly have given them my services as a nurse; but as they declined them, should I not open an Hotel for invalids in the Crimea in my own way?*[49] She was now seeing the British officials very differently. She would now proceed independently of them. As she argued, after all the authorities had hardly any more idea about her intended destination, the Crimea, than she had. So having made her mind up, she took the next positive step. She had cards printed and sent to her friends in the Crimea, which read:

BRITISH HOTEL
Mrs Mary Seacole
(Late of Kingston, Jamaica).
Respectfully announces to her former kind friends,
and to the Officers of the Army and Navy generally,
That she has taken her passage in the screw-steamer 'Hollander'
to start from London on 25th of January intending on her arrival
at Balaclava to establish a mess-table and comfortable quarters
for sick and convalescent officers.'

This was a truly bold venture and Mary estimated her cards

would arrive in the Crimea in about a week or so. The comforts of her hotel would be especially welcomed by the needy soldiers, many of whom were in poor accommodation.

As it was, luck smiled on Mary. While her new plan was maturing, she renewed her acquaintance with Mr. Day in England. It was her good fortune that he was on his way to Balaclava on shipping business. Mary laid her plans before him. He recognised her courage, enthusiasm and commitment, and, after some discussion, they agreed to open a store as well as a hotel near the camp. However fanciful it might have seemed, this was the origin of the firm of 'Seacole and Day.' But it was also the continuation of a relationship between Mary and Mr. Day that had started much earlier.[50] Important as these new arrangements were, Mary kept it separate from the main object of her voyage. With the help of a medical friend, most of her money was invested in medicines which she felt would be useful. What was left of her funds was spent on 'home comforts'.

The moment of truth had arrived: the time of departure was nigh. And so she boarded the *Hollander*, which left England on 27 January and sailed on with hope and great expectations. But once on board the ship, she was gripped by a pang of sadness. Just then, she said, she had met a friend who cheered her up as she gazed at the shores of England sinking beneath the sea. It was a bittersweet moment. Filled with private thoughts, she averted her gaze eastward as the ship plied its way towards Turkey.

Onward, At Last

The journey to Constantinople was, as Mary put it, 'interesting' and she boasted of being a good sailor. All the travelling she had previously done from Jamaica to Central America and to London now served her in good stead. Also in her favour was a robust constitution which helped her on the voyage during which the weather was fine generally. It was smooth sailing as each day diminished the doubts of success in Mary's mind. It was all real and happening. She was convinced of the rightness of what she was doing. It was a positive step towards achieving her goal.

When the ship stopped briefly at Gibraltar, Mary took advantage of spending a few hours on shore. Ever curious, one could imagine her vigilantly seeking the chance of a good deal. She could be likened to a latter-day 'shopaholic.' She was bargain-hunting and needed to be so inclined, for every moment from here on was an opportunity to stock up for her planned store. But instead of the bargains she was hoping to find at the foreign marketplace, she heard someone exclaim: *Why, bless my soul, old fellow, if this is not our good old Mother Seacole!* The voice came from a soldier whom Mary remembered from when he was in the 48th Regiment and had frequented her Kingston house. He was among the wounded men who had been invalided back from the Crimea. He was determined not to let her go without some socialising. Soon Mary, the solider and his friend were talking of old times over some *very nasty* wine. *And you are going to the front, old lady – you of all people in the world?* The soldier asked. *Why not my sons? Won't they be glad to have me there?'* Mary responded. Seeing her determination and hearing the strength and tone of her voice, the Irish soldier answered affirmatively, *By jove! Yes, mother,* The Irishman's response was not exaggerated, but quite genuine. Women were few and far between in these places and the wounded men were glad to have female company. They warmed to Mary's presence as most people did. As one of them put it: It isn't many women – God bless them – we've had to spoil us out there. *But it's not the place even for you, who know what hardship is. You'll never get a roof to cover you at Balaclava, nor on the road either.* Though she needed no reminding, they talked about some of the difficulties that awaited Mary. But such talk could not shake her resolve. *Do you think I shall be of any use to you when I get there?* Mary asked, and they replied: *Surely.*

Then I'll go, she said, *even if the place were a hundred times worse than you describe it.* Without compromising her femininity, Mary knew she had to be tough and adaptable to survive the remarkable journey she had undertaken. The line her finger had followed across the world map some months earlier, now looked very real. A realist, she recognised the necessity of sleeping rough, *on straw, like Margery Daw* as she put it.[51] Three years on, she remembered these soldiers' fondly, their merry laughter and good wishes for success in her plan. They also expressed concern for their friends and colleagues whom they had left behind. Before parting company with Mary, they expressed the hope of meeting her again. Like a much-needed tonic, this interlude on shore lifted Mary's spirits appreciably.

The ship's next stop was at Constantinople, where Mary's expectations were not met. She was clearly unimpressed. Put simply, she could not get on with the Turks she had met at the quayside. Amidst her trying moments, she had some luck in the form of news she had been expecting from someone. That person was Mr Day, whose letters had arrived at the local post office. Her expectations were dashed for she found that Mr. Day's news was not very good. His account of Balaclava and camp life was negative. There was no reason why Mary should not believe him and it almost convinced her that she should end her journey there. But while she was willing to allow intuition to play a significant part in her deliberations and decisions, now was the time for more reflection. Then, to her relief, she read Mr Day's instructions about the things that she should buy to advance their joint project and thus bring her closer to her objective. These crucial last words dispelled any doubts in Mary's mind. And so she set about her work which included making the purchases that Mr Day had recommended.

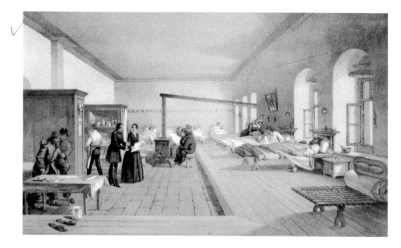

Florence Nightingale inspecting the wards of the Military Hospital at Scutari

Also in her possession at this time, was a letter of recommendation from a 'Dr F' which Mary carried on her way to the Scutari Hospital to see Miss Nightingale. What she could only have imagined way back in Jamaica and during her depressing, lonely days in London gave way to the reality that now appeared before her. The dull-looking hospital and the gloom and sadness amidst the rows of sick and dying made Mary tearful. She was, however, not without hope. After a while, in an environment which to some degree, she had recognised elsewhere, she was soon feeling better. Having scrutinised her surroundings, she described them thus: *The men were many of them very quiet. Some of the convalescent formed themselves into little groups around one who read a newspaper; others had books in their hands, or by their side, where they had fallen when slumber overtook the readers, while hospital orderlies moved to and fro, and now and then the female nurses in their quiet uniform, passed noiselessly on some mission of kindness.*[52]

Mary's reputation had preceded her. She came into contact with another of her 'old acquaintances' who guided her through the wards. She noted how busy the nurses, were as they attended to their urgent tasks. Her acquaintance was a 'Sergeant T' from the 97th Regiment whom she had known in Jamaica. He was recovering from dysentery and was eager to get back to the heat of battle. His delight in seeing Mary again was evident. He updated her on his life story and he took her to the sick beds of others she had known at home. It was an odd sight, but she was pleasantly surprised by the patients' response. The eyes of many glistened, she said, at the sight of the familiar face of an old friend in such an unlikely place as the Turkish barracks.

'Mother Seacole! Mother Seacole!' an excitable voice resounded. In turn, Mary warmed to it and offered a few words of comfort to the wounded man who had spoke. He became more excited when she told him she was on the way to the front. As a victim of scurvy and with confidence in her capabilities, he urged Mary to take vital supplies of vegetables and eggs that were so necessary to the well-being of the men at the front.

The awareness with which Mary approached her vocation of caring is reflected in her thoughts at this time. In spite of the risk of giving offence, she was unable to ignore the obvious need for helping hands in such situations. Until now, no one had been offended by either her actions or behaviour, but she thought she might have come close to doing so on one occasion when a doctor observed her actions: at first, she said he responded with surprise and alarm when she replaced a bandage. But when she was through, he thanked her politely.[53]

This affirmation of her skill and knowledge was timely for not only did she get the filip that she needed, but most importantly it came from an English doctor. It seems likely that had it come from someone of another nationality, it may well have had less impact upon her. Her sense of her Britishness, never in doubt, was, it seemed, now most pronounced. This experience further boosted her confidence. But although she was drawing ever closer, she was still not yet at the scene of war. Already forewarned by the *fearful miles* of suffering at the Scutari Hospital she wondered what it might be like closer to the front. For now, here at the hospital, the cries of pain and agony echoed about her as her soothing hands worked to bring relief. Nevertheless Mary felt she had to move on. There was no time to waste. It was about this time that she sought to present her letter of introduction to Florence Nightingale. After being guided along passages and corridors that were all used as sick wards, Mary eventually reached that section of the building known as the 'corner tower' which housed the nurses. Here, she met 'Mrs B', an official of some authority at the hospital who, as Mary put it, *felt more surprise than she could politely show* at her arrival. Unruffled by this, Mary handed Dr. F's letter to the woman who took it to Miss Nightingale. When she returned, she asked Mary to wait until Miss Nightingale was free to see her. While Mary waited, Mrs B, with the same look of curiosity and surprise, took the opportunity of putting more questions to her. Underlying all was the question: What was the purpose of Mrs Seacole coming out to that desolate place? Mary's answer was frank: *to be of use somewhere*. Mary gives us some idea of her dogged determination to be of assistance by her declaration that she would gladly work for the wounded in return for bread and water.

But Mary was saved from further thoughts of this kind when Mrs B, thinking that Mary sought employment at Scutari hospital said: *Miss Nightingale has the entire management of our hospital staff, but I do not think that any vacancy. . .* Before she could finish, Mary interrupted her: *Excuse me, ma'am, but I am bound for the Front in a few days.* Thus this interesting episode ended, but Mary noted that when Mrs B walked away, she looked even *more surprised than ever.* Mary waited for about half an hour before she was allowed to see Miss Nightingale. Face to face, it was a meeting of historic significance, for here were two women of their times, both motivated by a common cause – to serve Britain. They were 19th-century women from opposite ends of the socio-economic spectrum, one white from the heart of the Empire, the other black (or non-white) from a colonial backwater, one a pioneering paid administrator at the beginning of the new profession of nursing, the other a sutler (camp follower) who paid her own way and roughed it towards the war zone, one white and young, the other dark and much older. How did they perceive each other? In spite of their differences, this is how Mary described the English-woman whose reputation grew with each day: *A slight figure in the nurses' dress; with a pale, gentle and withal firm face, resting lightly in the palm of one white hand, while the other supports the elbow – a position which gives to her countenance a keen inquiring expression, which is rather marked. Standing thus in repose, and yet keenly observant – the greatest sign of impatience at any*

Florence Nightingale

time a slight perhaps unwitting motion of the firmly planted right foot – was Florence Nightingale – the Englishwoman whose name shall never die, but sound like music on the lips of British men until the hour of doom. From this description of the 'Lady with the Lamp', it seemed that even the 'Yellow doctress' was impressed by the appearance of the English nurse, whom she had heard of only very recently. But what was Miss Nightingale's response? According to Mary Seacole, Miss Nightingale read Dr F's letter which lay on the table beside her and in her *gentle but eminently practical and business-like way* she asked *what do you want Mrs Seacole – anything that we can do for you? If it lies in my power I shall be very happy.*[54] Although these words were well-received, as it was there was nothing that Miss Nightingale could do for Mrs Seacole. The fact remained that no offer of employment was made to her.

Mary's next request was of greater immediacy – a bed for the night. Why? Because she had missed the boat back to her ship and thought it was safer to spend the night at the Scutari Hospital. But even this request did not have the best of outcomes. Eventually a bed was found in the washerwoman's quarters. And as if that was not bad enough, that night proved to be most uncomfortable with fleas sharing her bed! After breakfast the next morning, Mary duly made her way back to the *Hollander*.

Once there, she transferred her things from the ship that had brought her thus far to the *Albatross*. This was a trying task for she had to overcome strong currents and hurricane winds, enduring an hour of *terrible anxiety and fear*, before she reached the *Albatross's* side. After her miserable night, she now had to climb on deck, *drenched and wretched*. To add to her anxiety were some bad news from Mr Day about the situation in Balaclava to which she was travelling. In these depressing circumstances, Mary was thankful that her companions were of a cheerful disposition and after the hazards of crossing the Black Sea, she described her excitement when she saw the rocky coast which heralded her arrival at Balaclava. The next morning, Mary was relieved by the order she found in Balaclava Harbour. She was filled with joy when Mr Day visited her on board the *Albatross*. This was the crucial moment when Mary said *our plans were laid*. She bade farewell to the *Albatross*, but until the future was decided upon in more detail with Mr Day, with no alternative lodgings, she took quarters on board the *Medora*, another ship which had been hired by Government at a great cost as an ammunition ship. Once she came to terms with her accommodation on the moored ship, the first thing Mary did was to let her friends know that she had moved to the Crimea and that their help was most welcome. At Balaclava, her earlier discomfiture was soothed by the pleasant surprises of re-acquainting herself with people she had known in Jamaica. Captain Peel, commander of the Naval Brigade, and Major-General Sir John Campbell were among those who welcomed her. They assured her of every assistance which was gratefully received, all the more because there was so much to do. She also met a man described *as poor H. Vicars, whose kind face had so often lighted up my old house in Kingston*. He took Mary by the hand and how odd and grateful Mary felt for his reassuring personality and presence in that *out of the way corner of the world*. Her confidence boosted, she declared *I never felt so sure of the success of my step as I did of this before I had been a week in Balaclava*. Nonetheless, she had plenty of difficulties on a range of matters in this foreign land.[55]

Having braved and survived the unpredictable sea, Mary's feet were once more firmly planted on dry land. The planning stages of her bold, imaginative Crimean enterprise had led to a new place and thus to the practicalities of the venture. By now she felt better prepared. During the six weeks of her stay in Balaclava, she spent her days on shore and her nights on board ship. It was a most unsettling, uncomfortable time, but there was no deviation from her objective. As her ideas crystallised, she recognised that a systematic approach was the only way forward. Each day, she apportioned time to receiving visitors and selling stores, but she never lost sight of the pressing humanitarian work of caring for the sick and dying. This, she regarded as her chief occupation on which there could be no compromise. Commenting on this, she wrote: . . . *I never allowed any business to interfere* [with] *helping the doctors to transfer the sick and wounded from the mules and ambulances into the transports that had to carry them to the hospitals of Scutari and Buyukdore. I did not forget the main object of my journey to which I would have devoted myself exclusively had I been allowed; and very familiar did I become before long with the Sick Wharf, a party of sick and wounded had just arrived.* Now the essential work for which she

Mary Seacole assisted with the embarkation of the wounded from the wharf at Balaclava for the Black Sea crossing to Scutari

had come had begun. Mary heard an artilleryman groaning and went to attend to him. He had been hit in the head. Mary *raised some tea to his baked lips . . . then his hand touched mine and rested there and I heard him mutter indistinctly, as though the discovery had arrested his wandering senses – Ha! This is surely a woman's hand.* In response, she spoke comforting words, then the wounded man whispered: *God bless you, woman, whoever you are, God bless you* over and over again. Once more Mary describes the effect of her presence upon others. She was there to help, but did she look the part of a nurse? Who could say? At the time nursing was in its infancy, just beginning to feel its way into becoming the vital profession it is now. Caring and saving lives were her primary concern in her early years in Jamaica and Central America, and was perhaps even more so now. And far from being a sprightly young nursing recruit, she was the opposite, popularly known as 'Mother' Seacole. It is perhaps this maturity and the vast experience that told against her application to go to the Crimea as a nurse. Apart from helping others, there was another side to Mary which hinted at self-satisfaction with her stout, round appearance, of which she was proud. If Mary was conspicuous by her physical presence, clearly, in a variety of ways, she was also the most colourful person around. *I do not think that the surgeons noticed me at first*, she explained, *although as this was my Introduction to Balaclava, I had not neglected my personal appearance and wore my favourite yellow dress and blue bonnet, with the red ribbons.*[56] It was not as though she was going to a picnic. The reason perhaps for wearing such feminine attire in such gaudy colours was its effect on the places she visited. She hoped it would lift the spirits of many around her who were clearly in need of a boost. Fortunately for them, Mary was not simply playing a part; it was in her character to be optimistic. All those who had met her, knew and felt this to be true, plus the fact that she was highly visible and unforgettable to those who had met her and benefited from her ministrations. To see her a second time and/or more frequently, especially amidst the heart-rending, bloody scenes in the war zone, was a bonus. Critics may well lambast her for over-playing her testimonials. But in her autobiography, she places before the reader eyewitness accounts instead of proclaiming her own interpretation of her actions. Among those who would later speak about her good deeds was a Captain, who became 'Major R' in charge of the wharf, from whom she had received a kind letter while at Balaclava. It read: *Dear Mrs Seacole, – I am very sorry to hear that you have been unfortunate in business; but I am glad to hear that you have found friends in Lord R----- and others, who are ready to help you. No one knows better than I do how much you did to help poor sick and wounded soldiers; and I feel sure you will find in your day of trouble that they have not forgotten it.* This was a promising start for Mary who regarded Major R's competence and sensitive approach towards the wounded very highly. Brave and experienced as the Major was, the tragedies he witnessed on the sick-wharf often *unmanned* him, she said. He worried a great deal about those in his charge. For Mary and the soldiers generally, such humanitarian concern was widespread. Nonetheless, she duly recognised the value of the care the women who served provided, a contribution which she said, few (if any) men could match. In respect of the need in the Crimea, the claims she made both in the West Indies, Central America and in London about the importance of her role in particular, but also of women generally were correct. In retrospect, she wrote: *Only women could have done more than they did who attended to this melancholy duty; and they, not because their hearts could be softer, but because their hands are moulded for this work.* So now amidst the smell of death, she did her best to help, even to effect some levity. As she informs us, there were some cheerful scenes at the sick wharf. In fact, the courage and magnanimity of spirit among the men was astonishing. She said they delighted in seeing her again so far from her native Jamaica, that idyllic tropical setting of their first meeting! At the sound of her name, she instantly recognised a sailor from her Kingston days. *'Why, as I live, if this ain't Aunty Seacole of Jamaica! Shiver all that's left of my poor timbers.'* The tone was reminiscent of the Irishman she had met when she stepped ashore in Gibraltar. On closer inspection, she realised the man's left leg was gone, yet, he kept his spirits up, *'if this ain't a rum go, mates!'*

Over the years, mixing with the English, Mary's use of English phrases and expressions had evolved to a point where she felt it was natural and fitting as she dealt with her 'sons.' *'Ah! My man, I'm sorry to see you in this sad plight.'*

'Never fear for me, Aunty Seacole; I'll make the best of the leg the Rooshians have left me. I'll get at them soon again, never fear. You don't think, messmates . . . that they'll think less of us at home for coming back with a limb or so short?'

'You bear your trouble well, my son,' Mary responded.

'Eh do I, Aunty?' he said with a look of surprise. *'Why look ye, when I've seen so many pretty fellows knocked off the ship's roll together, don't you think I ought to be thankful if I can answer the bo'swain's call anyhow?'*

Such courage as this man had shown affected the men as Mary related. *This brave fellow,* she said, *after he had sipped some lemonade and laid down, when he heard men groaning, raised his head and comforted them in the same strain again; and, it may seem strange, but it quieted them.* To comfort them in their last days and moments, Mary made and served the sick and wounded sponge-cakes and lemonade. Rising magnificently to the part and the occasion, like a mother, she watched over them and noted: *They all liked the cake, poor fellows, better than anything else: perhaps because it tasted of home.*[57] It was like home for Mary too, for now she was doing what she wholeheartedly did best: providing her special brand of care and concern always for those in need.

For some time yet, Mary lived aboard the ship, the *Medora*, to which she had been transferred. Whatever she may have imagined about life in Balaclava, it did not now surprise her. She had anticipated that life here would be rough. This was certainly the case for quite a while, days that were enough to try any woman's strength and nights during which she was not always certain of repose. For a woman, and one of her size and age (she was now about 50 years old), clambering up the sides of the ship each day was not easy. Why was it so difficult just to get on deck? The staves in the ladder, Mary explained, did not reach high enough and if they were broader that would have helped. Rarely did she complain, but this was not all that concerned her. Once aboard, there were other terrifying dangers. The *Medora* was an ammunition ship, packed with barrels of explosives – gunpowder and tons of cartridges – over which Mary and the ship's company slept. Given the volatile circumstances which justified its presence in that crowded harbour, the chances of this explosive cargo igniting were great.

Apart from sleepless nights, Mary was faced with the daytime worry of off-loading her stores with the help of Greek and Maltese boatmen, most of whom she described as professional thieves. If this was *harassing work*, even more so was the problem of protecting her property. For one thing, she could not conduct the surveillance of her property herself for here on the wharf, she not only sold 'stores,' but also administered medicines to those in need among the Land Transport and Army Works personnel. Thus, in spite of her best efforts, Mary was plagued by the ubiquitous thieves, prowling around especially at night. Their ingenuity was incredible, even worthy of admiration from Mary. *The thievery in this little out of the way post was something marvellous*, she later reflected, *and the skill and ingenuity of the operators would have reflected credit up the elite of the profession practising in the most civilised city in Europe.* Pragmatic and streetwise as Mary was, and as an observer of the customs and practice of different lands, thievery in this part of the world was widespread and on a different scale. The thieves' targets included the likes of Mary and the English, the Turks and one another. Mary was careful to distinguish between the Turks and others though, for they, as victims, received special treatment. She viewed the situation as being in a state of 'predatory warfare,' in which the French Zouaves were especially successful. She did not hide her admiration for these *brilliant little fellows*, a restless bunch, who, when denied access to the Russians, sought action in Balaclava. Their main interest was, according to Mary, to seek opportunities of *waging war against society at large*. Although they were indiscriminate in their thievery, with no regard for the property rights of others, Mary found it all quite amusing. Indeed, some two years later, she wrote about the thieves' artlessness which won her admiration. As she explained: *To see a Zouave gravely cheat a Turk or trip up a Greek street-merchant, or Maltese fruit-seller and scud away with the spoil, clearly stowed in his roomy red pantaloons, was an operation for its coolness, expedition and perfectness, well worth seeing. And, to a great extent, they escaped scatheless for the English Provost Marshall's department was rather chary of*

A sketch of Turkish Infantrymen in the Crimea by William Simpson

interfering with the eccentricities of our gallant allies. With each day, Mary's sympathy for the Turks grew. She thought it lamentable how they were robbed, abused and bullied and wondered why they did not show the fighting spirit of their compatriots by confronting their attackers. A little pluck and *ever so little spirit* was all they needed. But they would rather complain noisily and profusely instead of dealing with those who bullied them. It was rare that the tables were turned, and Mary only saw it happen once while she was there. She was still some distance away from the battle front, but it was clear to Mary that Balaclava was a dangerous place: *Had it not been for the unremitting activity of the authorities, no life would have been safe in Balaclava, with its population of villains of every nation. As it was, murder was sometimes added to robbery, and many of the rascals themselves died suspicious deaths, with the particulars of which the authorities did not trouble themselves.* In spite of it all, she recognised the efforts that went into maintaining law and order. Her experience at Balaclava taught Mary tough lessons, which served her in good stead for what was to come. Finally, after leaving Balaclava, Mary arrived at the spot where she desired to be, the place where *the necessary preparations in establishing her store were made.*[58] Her long-held dream of reaching the front in the Crimea was now reality.

Prelude to War

Before proceeding with Mary Seacole's story, let us consider the context of the Crimean War and the other women who were caught up in it. By 1853, the decline of the Ottoman Empire had become a matter of concern to the great powers of Europe. The ruler of Russia, Tsar Nicholas I, referring to the Ottomans, informed the British Ambassador that: 'We have a sick man on our hands, a man gravely ill, it will be a great misfortune if one of these days he slips through our hands, especially before the necessary arrangements are made.' Each of the major powers in Europe interpreted these 'necessary arrangements' in their own way. The Tsar, for example, was interested in control of Constantinople, which he saw as giving his fleet access to the warmer waters of the Mediterranean through the Bosphorous. Britain and France,

Tsar Nicholas I

already described as the 'policemen of Europe,' were also interested in territorial matters. Britain viewed Russian expansion in Asia and the Middle East as a threat to its interests in the Mediterranean and in India. And while France was keen to uphold its military prestige and further its imperial designs, Prince Albert reflected popular feeling when he said: 'The emperor of Russia is a tyrant and the enemy of all liberty on the Continent.'[59]

In the meantime, while the Ottoman Empire continued to decay, Russia and France, eager to extend their imperial interests, concentrated on the ongoing dispute concerning the rights of Christians to worship in Ottoman-ruled Jerusalem. Before 1850, Muslim policemen stood guard both inside and outside the Church of the Holy Sepulchre in Jerusalem, the Church of the Nativity in Bethlehem and the Tomb of the Virgin of Gethsemane in the hope of keeping peace between Catholics and Greek Orthodox Christians. This dispute was not as easy to resolve as it seemed and in time, it was used as a pretext for a much wider struggle, as Karl Marx put it. Historically, France regarded itself as the defender of Catholicism and priests and Christian places of worship. The Ottoman Empire's weakness helped matters little because both the French and Russian rulers felt they stood a real chance of winning the quarrel. A victory would settle the dispute. The subsequent 'war of words' drew all of Europe's great powers into diplomatic exchanges. In the ensuing negotiations, the three autocratic players, Tsar Nicholas I, Sultan Abdul Mejid and Napoleon III failed to agree. A short time later, the Tsar forced the issue by demanding the right to act on behalf of the millions of Orthodox Christians who were subjects of the Ottoman empire. This left little room for manoeuvre and the Tsar's ultimatum was turned down by the Sultan.

Russia responded in July 1853 by moving into the Ottoman Principalities of Moldova and Wallachia and on 5 October 1853 the Turks felt obliged to declare war against Russia. The Turkish Commander Omar Pacha served notice to Russia's General Gorchakov to leave the Principalities in two weeks. The Russians refused to comply and the Turks advanced on the Russians. The Turks won this confrontation. Nonetheless, the conflict persisted and the build-up of tension resulted in another confrontation, this time at sea. Both the Turkish and Russian fleets faced each other in the Black Sea, and in November 1853, the Russian Fleet destroyed a Turkish squadron in harbour at Sinope Bay, their use of explosive shells ushering in a new age of naval warfare and contributing to the end of the wooden warship. The Turkish defeat was on such a scale that in London, it was reported as a massacre. Lord Palmerston's response was that 'something must be done to wipe away the stain.' Thereafter, the Russian

Karl Heinrich Marx was born on 5 May 1818 in Trier in Germany. Forced to leave Germany in 1843 when his radical newspaper was suppressed, he met Friedrich Engels in Paris and it was here that he became a socialist. In 1848 the two men published *The Communist Manifesto*, but after the failure of the 1848 revolution Marx and his family moved to London, supported by the generosity of Engels who was working in his father's textile firm in Manchester. Marx's greatest work, *Das Kapital*, was written in London, where he died on 14 March 1883. He was buried in Highgate Cemetery.

Fleet sailed for Sebastopol and the British Admiralty began to consider attacking it. In Britain and France feelings ran high and rumours of war against Russia reached fever pitch. It was thought by many young men that should an attack take place, it would be a brief campaign and those who fought would be back home before Christmas. One of these young men was Private Timothy Gowing, a fusilier from Norwich: 'The Turks were trying to defend themselves against their ancient foes the Russians and thrilling accounts were appearing in our newspapers about the different fights at the seat of war on the Danube. I was now just approaching my twentieth year . . . and the accounts that were constantly coming home from the East worked me up to try my luck.'[60] And so just 40 years after Wellington had defeated Napoleon at Waterloo, France and Britain signed a military alliance. Finally, on 28 March 1854, they entered the war.

The Cabinet of Lord Aberdeen deciding upon the military expedition to the Crimea

Once war was declared, much attention shifted to the ordinary British soldier. If hitherto 'the profession of arms was still a worthy one for those who could purchase commissions, the soldier was [still] a social outcast,' a despised being, and the army was seen by its critics as a 'needless expense', a 'drag on the national economy.' Indeed, the private soldier found it useless to protest against the stigma of his lowly status. But now with the looming war, the 'popular mood underwent one of its many surprising changes. The despised redcoat was seen in a new light as war fever reached the level of hysteria . . . cheer boys, cheer.'[61] The British troops were the best-dressed expeditionary force ever: the Hussars, Light Dragoons, Heavy Dragoons and Lancers looked splendid. But it was argued that their regalia served no practical purpose. Moreover, the 'Army of the East' was hopelessly ill-equipped.

As the contingents marched out of their barracks on their way to the front, another surprising feature of the Crimean War was revealed, namely that behind each regiment came a company of women. Who were they? They were described as 'ill-assorted,' some as 'slatterns,' some with 'pinched' looks, some dressed in odd clothing, but most were 'wrapped in shawls.' Overall, they were a motley crew, among whom were 'gaunt and haggard faces; raw boned scrawny types that were almost devoid of sex; faces inured to hardship yet still in a mould of self respect.' As the men marched away, these hardened women followed. They tried to keep pace with the column, but some fell behind, while others were forced to trot. Determined, 'each woman carried a bundle which held all her possessions'. As it was, they were bound for a future where conditions, it was thought, could hardly be worse than those they were leaving behind. For they too were off to the 'Seat of War.' They were the Army wives and regimental women.

There were clear indications that the Army discouraged marriage among its non-commissioned ranks. The stone-barracks habitation of soldiers was no place for women and children. Commanding officers saw women as 'encumbrances' who detracted from the essentially displaced life of a soldier. Nonetheless, the presence of women could not be ruled out, 'even though little provision was made to settle them in quarters.'[62] By all accounts, life in the barracks was appalling. According to Compton: 'The atmosphere of the large unventilated rooms, kept airless for the sake of warmth was frequently poisoned by badly positioned drains. The death rate from tuberculosis among soldiers . . . was five times as great as among civilians. These were the conditions in which married soldiers and their wives set up their homes, separated one from another by flimsy curtains or, if they were lucky, in a corner where screens might deaden the sights, but not the sounds or smells of a never-empty barrack room. The fact that there was little prospect of improvement made these surroundings all the more depressing.

To compound the problems of the soldier and his wife, consider the pay of one shilling which a private received each week.

From this, 6d a week was deducted 'for rations, replacements and a never ending list of extras,' which meant a severe reduction of a couple's budget. It was here, as one historian put it, that the soldiers wife came in useful. For in return for their higgledy-piggledy space in barracks, the wives were granted the 'privilege' of doing the job of washerwomen for the troops. Other wives chose to be, or were employed as, cooks or seamstresses. Some were picked to be nursemaids in officers' families and were regarded as a 'better' type of regimental woman. Generally though, most of these women worked in the barracks' laundries. With time, they became so toughened that they gained a reputation for being 'rough and ready' travellers. Yet it was found, and surprisingly so, 'that some barrack women retained their innate sterling qualities of proper pride, loyalty and devotion so that they were fully conversant with 'the spirit of the Regiment to which they belonged.' Nonetheless, their numbers were limited for according to the Queen's Regulations, an average of six wives was permitted for each company of 100 infantrymen. Many wives were so determined to join their husbands that they pleaded with officers' wives to employ them as 'maids.'[63]

And so, for better or worse, many women followed their men to the Crimean war. Early in 1854, we can picture the following scene. The Coldstream Guards' departure from St George's barracks was an emotional one, which greatly affected the crowds that had gathered on the steps of St. Martin's Church and filled Trafalgar Square. Among the column of men that marched by were an estimated 32 women. The barracks vacated by the Coldstreams were, in turn, occupied by the Grenadier Guards from the Tower, who were expected to leave the next day at noon. The excitement among them was such that it was said none of them slept that night. One historian, Piers Compton described what happened next: 'Tatoo sounded but no one interfered though the barrack room was filled with the men and their women-folk.

At 3am the bugle sounded the roll call and companies fell in under the dim yellow light of a lantern. Two hours later, the leading files emerged through the West door of the National Gallery and once again the thoroughfares from Charing Cross and

Grenadiers Guards bound for the Crimea march through Trafalgar Square. 22 February 1854

Waterloo Bridge rocketed into life.' Amidst renditions of 'Rule Britannia' and 'God Save the Queen,' there were patriotic shouts of 'Grenadiers remember England,' as the Grenadiers marched towards Whitehall. Then, as 'Annie Laurie' was played people sang along and a 'little muster' of about 20 regimental wives did their best to keep pace with the troops as they marched past the Palace. One reporter, who took a keen interest in these women wrote: 'The married women who [accompanied] the soldiers [can] easily be distinguished from their less fortunate companions by being laden like pack horses.' That same month, a few hundred miles away at Plymouth Quay, a more fortunate couple, Captain and Fanny Duberly embarked on the *Shooting Star*. In their wake, one nagging question remained: were the women of the Army 'more to be pitied than the Regimental wives' who chose to remain in England? Compton informs us of the desperation among Army wives who were left behind for whom there was 'no allowance nor provision whatever.' In the absence of their husbands and without the means of any income, they were 'unable to keep up a regular home even if they had one, and often with children to support, their survival becomes a mystery.' Thus many wives had no option but either to turn to the local work-house or starve.[64] But while many excluded Army wives faced a bleak future at home, those thought to have been more fortunate by being in the transport ships had to endure agonies of discomfort before they experienced the hellish conditions of camp life on and near the battlefields of the Crimea.

Against this background of British women from the heart of the Empire who made their way to the war zone, Mary Seacole was conspicuous not only by her colourful dress, skill and age, but also because she was a woman of colour from a far-flung outpost of the Empire. But now here she was among the 'British' women, having arrived at the place where she would begin the process of building her British Hotel.

The British Hotel

The moment of truth for making the 'British Hotel' a reality had arrived. Of course, Mary could not have known at the time (or did she?) that this would be the beginning of a project that was to become a monument to her presence and multifaceted work in the Crimea. Starting from scratch in this new environment, the location called Spring Hill had its own pit-falls as Mary now set about the task of erecting the Hotel. Finding her bearings was essential. How did she get around? She informs us that she did so sometimes on horseback, sometimes getting a lift on the commissariat carts and occasionally on the ammunition railway wagons. She visited Spring Hill every day and, out of necessity, a shed to accommodate her was erected. Soon she began to realise the enormity of what she had got herself into. In the circumstances, the difficulties that constructing the Seacole and Day Hotel presented were clearly immense. For one thing, acquiring building materials was a major problem, *next to impossible*, she said. She resorted to collecting what she could find, including bits and pieces of driftwood and timber from the harbour along the harbour. She then faced the task of hiring workmen. Eventually, she was able to assemble a group of workmen among whom were two English sailors, nicknamed 'Big and Little Chips' and some Turks.

While gathering her workforce, she had made the acquaintance of the 'Pacha,' Commander of the Turkish division encamped near Spring Hill. With materials and men gathered together, building commenced, but the process proved to be far from easy or smooth. Unforseen circumstances tested her often.

On one occasion, heavy rains burst a dam, creating a deluge which swept along Spring Hill with disastrous results. Mary's 'temporary hut' was flooded and stores of up to £200 in value were destroyed. But characteristically, because Mary was unwilling to part with some of her belongings, the torrent that hit Spring Hill could have been tragic for her. Later she reflected that *after seeing a little box which contained some things, valuable as relics of the past, being carried away, I plunged in after it and losing my balance, was rolled over and over by the stream, and with some difficulty reached the shore.* Without questioning her fearlessness and impulsiveness, could this passage be a retrospective exaggeration? The next day, the building site looked a sad wreck, which won the sympathy and help of British commander Lord Raglan's men who were passing by.

In time, Mary Seacole realised the importance of establishing local contacts, and soon her friendship with the Pacha grew stronger. Indeed their relationship was so warm that some in

Born in 1788, Fitzroy James Henry Somerset, 1st Baron Raglan, was commissioned in the British Army in 1804, and served throughout Wellington's campaigns in the Peninsula and at Waterloo in 1815, where he lost an arm. The Duke's military secretary until his death in 1852, Raglan was highly valued for his administrative skills, tact and urbanity. These qualities lead to him being chosen to command the army sent to the Crimea in 1854 to co-operate with the French and the Turks. Raglan became the scapegoat for the many failings of the Allied expedition, and worn out and ill, he died in the camp outside Sebastopol on 28 June 1855.

Spring Hill felt the Pacha was showing unusual interest in her. But with three wives, Mary felt he had no need for another one. The Turkish Commander's greatest desire, she explained, was to be familiar with the English language, and, to this end, he turned to Mary for guidance and help. He would try hard *to sow a few English sentences in his treacherous memory*, but his progress was slow. He tried harder, but could only manage about half a dozen sentences, and Mary was convinced that had they continued their pupil/teacher relationship, there would have been no significant progress in spite of the Pacha's best efforts. But although he was clearly not destined for linguistic excellence, the Pacha maintained warm and friendly relations with Mary and often his band provided the music at Spring Hill. Such interludes soothed the jangled nerves of her customers, which Mary appreciated. In time, she came to regard this Turkish gentleman as *a capital neighbour* whose rank and orders afforded her the protection she so clearly needed. Yet, the thieves were never far away. Naturally, she was sad to see the Pacha and his men depart for Kamara. The loss of her Turkish neighbours was a blow felt in more ways than one. For quite a while, Mary felt exposed on Spring Hill. It was only when men of the Land Transport Corps encamped near Mary's land that she felt reasonably safe. How she wished she

Lord Raglan conferring with his allies, Omer Pacha and General Pelissier

could see more of her business partner Mr Day, who, she said rarely returned to Spring Hill until nightfall. This meant that his responsibilities were left unfulfilled. Nonetheless, Mary did the best she could to make progress. The necessary assistance she received came from those she had recruited. She kept on by sheer determination and courage and *a poor delusion which I took care to heighten by the judicious display of a double-barrelled pistol, lent me for the purpose by Mr Day and which I couldn't have loaded to save my life.*[65]

So Mary had to be necessarily vigilant as she supervised the building of the British Hotel. As the end of the summer months approached, the project was almost complete. But Mary even months later reflected that the Hotel *never was completed and when we left the Hill . . . it still wanted shutters.* Yet, it was regarded by all as the most complete thing there. At a cost of some £800, the British Hotel and its surrounding buildings covered about an acre of land. It was as perfect as they could make it, Mary insisted. She described the Hotel and storehouse thus: . . . *a long iron room, with counters, closets and shelves; above it was another room, used by us for storing our goods and above this floated a large Union Jack. Attached to this building was a little kitchen, not unlike a ship's caboose – all stoves and shelves. In addition to the iron-house were two wooden houses, with sleeping apartments for myself and Mr Day, outhouses for our servants, a canteen for the soldiery and a large enclosed yard for our stock, full of stables, low huts and sties. Everything although rough and unpolished was comfortable and warm; and there was a completeness about the whole which won general admiration.*[66]

Gazing at the Hotel, what satisfaction must Mary have felt. She was the woman who foresaw this need. She was the right woman, in the right place at the right time. Despite mismanagement and problems in the camp, she now had a clearer view of why she was there. Within her own sphere of influence, she was determined to bring comfort and order at Spring Hill. In the days that passed, those who visited the Hotel were refreshed. Encouraged, Mary was careful to spare no expense in stocking her store with everything *from an anchor down to a needle*. The most pressing problem, as previously, was that of thieves, who kept an eye out for anything and everything which they felt could be lifted. While she braved the Crimean cold and rainy weather, it was the thieves who posed the greatest threat. No wonder that Mary felt besieged by thieves, both human and animal – the rats. She tried to combat the thieves, but the extent of thievery was overwhelming and cost her dearly. As she put it: *Although we kept a sharp look-out by day and paid a man five shillings a night as watchman, our losses were very great. During the time we were in the Crimea, we lost over a score of horses, 4 mules, 80 goats, many sheep, pigs and poultry by thieving alone! We missed in a single night 40 goats and 7 sheep, and on Mr Day's going to headquarters with intelligence of the disaster, they told him that Lord Raglan had recently received 40 sheep from Asia, all of which had disappeared in the same manner. The geese, turkeys and fowls vanished by scores.*[67]

Mary worried about her livestock and food stores, but she also needed to ensure her personal safety. And with good reason: she wrote about her fears at Spring Hill, after the brutal murder of her washer-woman and all her seven children. The whole camp was stunned and Mary's fears increased because the murderer, or murderers, were still at large. Mary's losses from theft were, at times, serious. Among the items taken from her stock were table cloths, domestic linen and most of her clothes. Fortunately, she was able to buy more.[68] Nonetheless Mary Seacole, the opportunistic, multi-talented businesswoman, proceeded to engage in what she had come out to the Crimea to do.

Following the opening that summer of the Seacole and Day establishment, as winter approached, even though roaring winds and rain played havoc and made roads impassable, officers found their way to the Hotel. Shortages were glaringly obvious, namely the want of shirts and socks, pocket handkerchiefs and wrapping paper. Mary also realised that the acquisition of a number of things were necessary for her to truly deliver the home comforts which she promised the soldiers who congregated at Spring Hill, which became synonymous with the British Hotel. Hungry officers made their way along muddy roads to see what Mother Seacole had in store. Her cooking, either for lunch or dinner, was eagerly anticipated by many who had become regulars. Meat, meat-pies, rice puddings, pastry and rhubarb tarts were among the things she served up for her 'sons'. *I declare I never heard or read of an Army so partial to pastry as the British Army before Sebastopol.*[69] Indeed it was not unusual to see a crowd of officers, in high spirits in the kitchen of Mary's Hotel. Sometimes when their behaviour had tested her sorely, she was known to brandish an iron spoon in frustration. At such times, the *good-for-nothing* black cooks stood about laughing with *all their teeth*. Mary Seacole's establishment became a popular meeting place, a haven of rest and pleasure. In the hot weather, many flocked to the Hotel especially for Mary's specials: claret and cider cups and other cooling drinks. Mary spoke a good deal about mothering the men, ensured that they had adequate and well-prepared food. And, often when she related how funny some things were, she did not neglect the tragic side also.

As she began to find her feet, so to speak, in that new and dangerous environment, what must it have been like? In her autobiography, she begged the reader's permission before describing one day of her life in the Crimea: *I was generally up and busy by day-break, sometimes earlier, for in the summer my bed had no attractions strong enough to bind me to it after four! There was plenty to do before the work of the day began. There was the poultry to pluck and prepare for cooking, which had been killed the previous night; the joints to be cut up and got ready for the same purpose; the medicines to be mixed; the store to be swept and cleaned. Of very great importance, with all these things to see after, were the few hours of quiet before the road became alive with*

travellers. By 7 o'clock the morning coffee would be ready, hot and refresh-
ing and eagerly sought for by the Officers of the Army Works Corps. . . .
There was always a great demand for coffee by those who knew its refresh-
ing and strengthening qualities, milk I could not give them (I kept tins
for special use); but they had it hot and strong, with plenty of sugar and
a slice of butter, which I recommend as a capital substitute for milk. From
that time until nine, officers on duty in the neighbourhood, or passing by,
would look in for breakfast and about half-past nine my sick patients
began to show themselves. In the following hour they came thickly and
sometimes it was past twelve before I had got through this duty. They came
from every variety of suffering and disease; the cases I most dislike were
the frost-bitten fingers and feet in the winter. That over, there was the
hospital to visit across the way, which was sometimes overcrowded with
patients . . . I used not always to stand upon too much ceremony when I
heard of sick or wounded officers in the Front. Sometimes their friends
would ask me to go to them, though very often I waited for no hint, but
took the chance of meeting with a kind reception. I used to think of their
relatives at home, who would have given so much to possess my privilege;
and more than one officer have I startled by appearing before him, and
telling him abruptly that he must have a mother, wife or sister at home
whom he missed, and that he must therefore be glad of some woman to take
their place.[70]

Then as the day neared its end, she tells us: *Until evening the*
store would be filled with customers wanting stores, dinners and lunch-
eons; loungers and idlers seeking conversation and amusement; and at
eight o'clock the curtain descended on that day's labour and I would sit
down and eat at leisure. It was no easy thing to clear the store, canteen
and yards; but we determined upon adhering to the rule that nothing
should be sold after that hour, and succeeded. Anyone who came after that
time, came simply as a friend! There could be no necessity for anyone,
except on extraordinary occasions, when the rule could be relaxed, to
purchase things after eight o'clock. And drunkenness or excess were dis-
couraged at Spring Hill in every way; indeed my few unpleasant scenes

arose chiefly from my refusing to sell liquor where I saw it was wanted to be abused! I could appeal with a clear conscience to all who knew me there, to back my assertion that I neither permitted drunkenness among the men nor gambling among the officers. Whatever happened elsewhere, intoxication, cards and dice were never to be seen within the precincts of the British Hotel. At first, we kept our store open on Sunday from sheer necessity, but after a little while, when stores in abundance were established at Kadikoi and elsewhere, the absolute necessity no longer existed, Sunday became a day of most grateful rest at Spring Hill. This step also met with opposition from the men; but again we were determined and again we triumphed. I am sure we needed rest . . . although I never had a week's illness during my campaign the labour, anxiety and perhaps the few trials that followed it, have told on me. I have never felt since that time the strong hearty woman that I was when I braved with impunity the pestilence of Navy Bay and Cruces. It would kill me easy now.[71]

Amidst the Carnage

In her autobiography, Mary Seacole wrote that she feared seeming self-congratulatory in giving an account of her work in the Crimea, although her achievement in reaching the front at all against overwhelming odds would make some self-congratulation seem justified. *I enter upon the particulars of this chapter of my life with great reluctance*, she admitted, *but I cannot omit them for the simple reason that they strengthen my one and only claim to interest the public, viz, my services to the brave British Army in the Crimea.* However, the fact that there was no shortage of other people to bear testimony to her work made it unnecessary for her to blow her own trumpet. Thus she wrote: *I can put on record the written opinions of those who had ample means of judging and ascertaining how I fulfilled the great object which I had in view of leaving England for the Crimea.* But before doing so she felt it was important to solicit her readers' attention to her position in the camp as doctress, nurse and 'mother.' In the world of the mid-19th century, with war and sickness so widespread, Mary had always found her experience and practice of medical art useful wherever she went. Even in London, she had found her knowledge and skills to be of service to others. This was an area of nursing in which she was fully competent and confident of her abilities. But she can hardly have imagined the conditions she found in the war zone. The Crimea was a strange place, a surreal scene of death and destruction of such magnitude that doctors were *so overworked and sickness was so prevalent that I could not be long idle; for I never forgot that my intention in seeking the Army was to help the kind-hearted doctors, to be useful to them for I have ever looked upon and still regard it as so high a privilege.* If she felt ennobled in their company, amidst the carnage and confusion, soon Mary was surrounded by patients of her own, aiding the regimental doctors whose surplus patients found their way to the British Hotel daily for treatment and nourishing food. With no competing establishment, she made herself known and useful to an ever-growing clientele. Her easy and welcoming manner cheered the officers and men who saw her as warm and caring, and they were not only reassured by her strong, stout motherly frame, but also by the fact that she was a 'doctress and nurse.' If they did not know it at first, as each day passed the soldiers realised that she never tired in her concern for them. Instead of remaining in their cheerless huts, Mary welcomed them to partake of her home comforts. With hindsight, she painted a picture of gloom, of stark realism for readers of her *Wonderful Adventures…* in England. She asked them to consider *lying with parched lips and fading appetite thousands of miles from mother, wife or sister, loathing the rough food by your side and thinking regretfully of that English home where nothing that could minister to your great need would be left untried.* Ever on the move, often on horseback, she went beyond the call of duty to please the British officers and men. She fed, bandaged and applied her healing art: gave them food and drink, applied soothing hands with whispered words to comfort them. Predictably, her humanitarian concern took its toll. Over the days and months of witnessing and feeling deep pain her face became more careworn, the lines on her forehead more pronounced. But advancing age was no deterrent. She was ubiquitous, spreading her much-appreciated cheerfulness, her smile like rays of sunlight through the gloom and depression that hung over the area like a cloud. She was now perhaps the best-known of all those in Spring Hill and its ravaged environs. In such circumstances, she wrote, *don't you think that you would welcome the familiar figure of the stout lady whose bony horse has just pulled up at the door of your hut, and whose panniers contain some cooling drink, a little broth, some homely cake or a dish of jelly or blancmange.*[72] The famous British magazine *Punch* agreed with Mary Seacole and famously remarked:

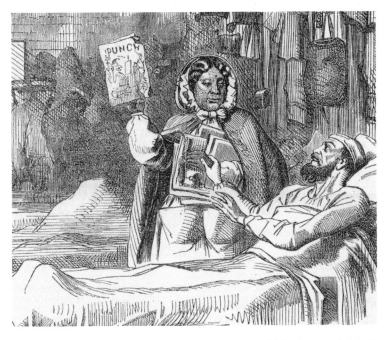

An illustration of Mary Seacole nursing in the Crimea, published in *Punch*. 1857

'that berry-brown face, with a kind heart's trace
Impressed on each wrinkle sly,
Was a sight to behold, though the snow-clouds rolled
Across the iron sky.'[73]

So Mary Seacole's bright personality lit up the place, giving a welcoming, homely feel in this war-torn outpost. She said she had seen many *a bold fellow's eyes moisten* on hearing a woman's voice and on receiving a woman's care which, she said, reminded them of *happy English homes which some of them never saw again; but many did, who will remember their woman-comrade upon the bleak and barren heights before Sebastopol.* She drew great satisfaction when she remembered them calling her 'mother.' In turn, these patriots were her 'sons,' who were susceptible to things that triggered memories of home. Among her patients in the Crimea, was one whom she had known in Jamaica, a winner of the Victoria Cross, who was cured by her caring hands. Later, in her autobiography, she reproduced two letters from a patient who had suffered from jaundice to whom she recommended medicine which made him feel better.

My Dear Mrs Seacole,

I have finished the bottle, which has done my jaundice a deal of good. Would you kindly send another by bearer. Truly yours, 'F.M'.

Mary adds: *It was a capital prescription which had done his jaundice good. There was so great a demand for it, that I kept it mixed in a large pan, ready to ladle it out to the scores of applicants who came for it.*[74] She said her heart bled for the suffering men to whom she played hostess at the British Hotel.

Thus far, Mary had given her readers a good idea of her life in the Crimea; and writing several months later, she offered three excuses for any *historical inexactness*. First, her memory was unreliable and she had no written record; second that although the reader would have had enough of journals and chronicles of Crimean life, she was unique in being the only historian of Spring Hill and third, unless she was allowed to tell her story in her own way, she would not tell it at all. We already know what her life was like at the British Hotel, but what was her life like out of doors, on the field of battle? She bore witness to and was humbled as the great events unfolded. But in recording what she saw, inevitably, there were gaps because she could not be everywhere. Her absence from the scene of memorable actions were attributed both to her attendance to the stricken and wounded and because she was either *mixing medicines or making good things* in the kitchen of the British Hotel. Although she was in the Crimea and knew a great deal about the battle of Tchernaya, she did not see it from the vantage point of a hill top. Even regarding this experience, she was aware of the discrepancy between being on the spot or near the scene of action and reading about it from afar, shortcomings of which she wrote that the news which created *so much sensation in England, was but little regarded at Spring Hill.*[75]

The occupation of the Tchernaya lines, 25 May 1855, from a drawing by Lebreton

Her first experience of Battle was *pleasant enough*. After all, this was why she came, to witness and partake in camp life and the *pomp, pride and circumstance of glorious war*. Sitting on her horse she enjoyed the amazing sight of English, French and Turkish forces over the plain. How *pretty* it was to see the clouds of smoke from behind the bushes answered by fire from the other side in skirmishes. *This was my first experience of actual Battle*, she wrote, *and I felt that strange excitement which I do not remember on future occasions, coupled with an earnest longing to see more of warfare and to share in its hazards. It was not long before my wish was gratified.*[76]

Mary revelled in danger. All that she had dreamed about was now reality. She was in the midst of it all, although she admitted to knowing very little about the second bombardment of Sebastopol in April. From her position on Spring Hill she was able to judge the severity of the battle by the long trains of wounded which passed by the British Hotel. True to her character, the ever-ready Mary had a stretcher laid near her door, because very often a poor fellow was laid upon it, exhausted by his terrible journey from the field. The bombardment was unsuccessful and after it, according to Mary, there was a sudden lull in the siege during which she received a number of visitors, including Florence Nightingale who had come to supervise the Balaclava hospitals. Before long, Mary had indeed gained practical experience of the Crimean fever!

Florence Nightingale was born on 12 May 1820, and devoted her life to charitable work. A good organiser, she was superintendent of the Institute for Sick Governesses in Harley Street when in 1854 the public outcry at the suffering in the Crimea lead the Secretary of War to call upon her to lead a party of 38 nurses to go to the hospital at Scutari. Here her role was mainly administrative, though she did visit wards, earning her title of 'the Lady with the Lamp'. After the war she continued to work for the welfare of troops and better nursing standards. She died in London on 13 August 1910.

In the wake of the revered Lady of the Lamp (as Florence Nightingale became known), there were other illustrious people who passed Mary's way, such as the Duke of Newcastle and Monsieur Alexis Soyer whom Mary described as *the great high priest of the mysteries of cookery*, a regular at Spring Hill. The greeted each other warmly on their first meeting. Soyer describes it thus: 'As I was not well acquainted with the high road across the country, I made up my mind to follow the high one which passes close to head-quarters. When about halfway, I perceived a group of officers standing by the roadside round a kind of tent much like a gypsy tent. I was riding towards it when much to my astonishment, several voices called out – "Soyer! Soyer! Come here – come this way!" I readily complied with the invitation and found two of the gentlemen whom I had the pleasure of knowing. During our conversation, an old dame of a jovial appearance, but a few shades darker than the white lily, issued from the tent, bawling out, in order to make her voice heard above the noise, "Who is my new son?" to which one of the officers replied, "Monsieur Soyer, to be sure; don't you know him?"

"God bless me, my son, are you Monsieur Soyer of whom I heard so much in Jamaica? Well, to be sure! I have sold many a score of your Relish and other sauces – god knows how many".[77]

Mary invited Soyer to join Sir John Campbell in taking a glass of champagne and as she went to fetch the drink, Campbell explained to Soyer who she was. In turn Soyer was equally impressed with the 'celebrated Mrs Seacole' as she was with him. Although Soyer had written his description of her after the war when she had achieved celebrity status, Soyer gave the impression that she was already a popular figure before her British Hotel fame. When Mary reappeared with the bottles to treat the gentlemen, Monsieur Soyer recalled the moment:

'We all declared it would never do for a lady to stand treat in the Crimea.

"Lord bless you, Monsieur Soyer," said the lady, "Don't you know me?"

"Yes, I do now, my dear Madam."

"Well, all those fine fellows you see here are my Jamaica sons – are you not?" said she, opening the champagne and addressing the General.

"We are Mrs Seacole and a very good mother you have been to us".[78]

They then drank a toast to each other.

Mary described the celebrated chef as having the *most smiling of faces and* [wearing] *the most gorgeous of irregular uniforms and*

The flamboyant chef Alexis Benoit Soyer was born on 4 February 1810. In 1837 he was appointed Chef at the Reform Club in London, where he installed modern kitchens and was one of the first to use gas for cooking. His books included *A Shilling Cookery for the People* (1855) and *A Culinary Campaign* (1857). He accompanied Florence Nightingale to the Crimea and organised catering at the hospitals. The field stove he designed at this time was so efficient and economical that it remained in service for at least a century. He died in London on 5 August 1858.

never failed to praise my soups and dainties. But she fancied herself as a good cook too. *I always flattered myself that I was his match and with our West Indian dishes could of course beat him hollow, and more than once I challenged him to a trial of skill; but the gallant Frenchman only shrugged his shoulders and disclaimed my challenge with many flourishes of his jewelled hands, declaring that Madame proposed a contest where victory would cost him his reputation for gallantry and be more disastrous than defeat. And all because I was a woman forsooth.* This kind of talk annoyed Mary Seacole, who always spoke up for herself. *What nonsense,* she answered, *to talk like that when I was doing the work of half a dozen men.* Nonetheless, her sense of humour got the better of her. She, in turn, recognised the Frenchman's good-humour and declared that *when our* [Crimean] *campaigns were over we would render rivalry impossible, by combining to open the first restaurant in Europe. There was always fun in the store when the good-natured Frenchman was there.*[79]

Mary's love for, and close association with, soldiers was such that at a moment's notice she was willing to help the First Regiment of Sardinian Grenadiers who stayed at Spring Hill overnight on their way to their positions. By now, it seemed that Mary Seacole's well-founded fear of thievery and thieves had somewhat receded. She was her trusting self again. And fortunately for her and the Regiment, not a single item was stolen that night. She marvelled at this all the more because there was no lack of opportunities for the thieves. The war in the Crimea brought many visitors from all over the world to make Spring Hill their headquarters. All sorts of people came and went and not surprisingly, among them was a 'swindler,' a Captain St. Clair whom Mary nonetheless treated well. She gave to him the best of everything. Even in such unfortunate circumstances, the goodness of her heart shone through for she later wrote of him as a man of some substance, whom she appreciated. It was this big-heartedness, a capaciousness of spirit and humanity that set her apart from others in the Crimea. Mary was also re-acquainted with another 'visitor' to the camp in the Crimea – namely cholera, of which she had had a good deal of experience. Such a visitation at such a time was most unwelcome.

As preparations got under way for the third 'great bombardment' of the city, the summer sunshine broke through beautifully and, for a while, visitors to the Seacole and Day British Hotel were relaxed and cheerful. It was remarkable how quickly moods changed. In this brief period, amusement was the order of the day – races, hunts, cricket matches and dinner parties and, as it got hotter, Mary prepared her own popular brand of cooling beverages for friends and customers. The variety of what she presented to the soldiers and officials must have been, apart from taste, most pleasing to the eye. No wonder her sangaree, claret, cider cups and ices went down well! How precious these times were, for soon the bombardment and loss of life would come again. And when it did, it was with renewed and unforgettable ferocity. As she reminded readers of her autobiography *although there might be only a few short and sullen roars of the great guns by day, few nights passed without some fighting in the trenches.* The cost was great and in many cases deeply personal for Mary. *Very often,* she wrote, *the news of the morning would be that one or other of those I know had fallen.* This affected her deeply and often she would wake up in the night and hear the thundering of guns. Day after day, she dreaded the sadness that the dawn would bring. Although bad news was something she had lived with from time to time, it was never easy for her to be the bearer of such news. While she went about her business in a cheerful manner, the certainty of death in the trenches haunted her. Why? She explains. Because *it was very usual, when a young officer was ordered into the trenches, for him to ride down to Spring Hill to dine or obtain something more than his ordinary fare to brighten his dreary hours in those fearful ditches*, which quickly became graves. Farewells and goodbyes before battles were always sad, poignant reminders of her time in the Crimea. Of the young officers she had known, she wrote: *They seldom failed on these occasions to shake me by the hand at parting, and sometimes would say, 'You see, Mrs Seacole, I can't say goodbye to dear ones at home, so I'll bid you good-bye for them. Perhaps you'll see them someday, and if the Russians should knock me over, mother, just tell them I thought of them all – will you?' And although all this might be said in a light-hearted manner, it was rather solemn! I felt it to be so, for I never failed (although who was I, that I should preach?) to say something about God's Providence and relying upon it; and they were very good! No Army of parsons could be much better than my sons.* In turn, they regarded Mary as their 'Mother.' She was now known as the 'Mother of the Army.' They were unusually attentive and as they shook her hand, she was overwhelmed by her feelings for them. She reflected too upon the private soldiers who would often say *I'm going in with my Master tonight Mrs Seacole; come and look after him if he is hit.* And sure enough when they left her, she would spend a restless night and an anxious morning waiting for the dreaded news. It had become so personal that she was moved to write *I used to think it was like having a large family of children ill with fever and dreading to hear which one had passed away in the night.* In the aftermath, the dutiful Mary felt bound to go up to the hut of the wounded and or sick and do her *woman's work,* to which she was fully committed. *How could it be otherwise?* she questioned. She remembered the dead and dying faces of many boys and men, including old Jamaica friends, one of whom was a *great character.* Reflecting upon these sorrowful occasions, Mary was nevertheless quick to point out that amidst the carnage and suffering, there was little time for grieving. As an eye-witness and participant in the Crimean War, hitherto, she pointed out that in relation to the horrors of the fatal trenches, the real history had never been written. But, she added, *it is as well that so harrowing a tale should be left in oblivion.* Of those trenches she told the story of two sergeants, schoolmates who had lost track of each other, until by different routes, they met again in, of all places, the trenches, *under the fire of a common enemy.* When they recognised each other, they raced forward and with hearty handshakes, they exchanged mutual greetings. *While their hands were still clasped*, they were both shot and killed.[80]

If what she had related above was bad, there was worse to come as she picked her way through the dangerous Crimean battlefield. She referred to a testimonial from the Adjutant-General of the British Army in which he stated that Mary had often done the best she could, attending to the wounded men regardless of situations of great danger. Discharging her strong sense of duty, frequently under fire, was paramount to Mary. Danger was endemic in her work and soon, she said, it failed to *create more than temporary uneasiness.* To illustrate her point, she stated that *after Sebastopol was ours, you might often see officers and men strolling coolly, even leisurely across and along those streets, exposed to the enemy's fire, when a little haste would have carried them beyond the reach of danger. The truth was, I believe, they had grown so habituated to being in peril from shot and shell that they rather liked the sensation and found it difficult to get on without a little gratuitous excitement and danger.* At this crucial time of the Crimean campaign, Mary was clearly involved in serious engagements that exposed her to considerable peril. Indeed, the situation was so risky that one could hardly move around the different camps. At times, the enemy was far too close for comfort. Russian shot had not only struck huts and tents, but also on one occasion when Mary was on her horse, one landed almost immediately in front of her.[81]

Allied batteries besieging the city of Sebastopol

When eventually the third bombardment of Sebastopol began in the height of summer, the Spring Hill visitors had plenty to talk about. According to Mary, many people guessed when the attack against the Russians would commence. But no one doubted the success of this campaign. As planning of the bombardment continued important secrets *oozed out* from various places, one of which was the British Hotel. During the run-up to the attack, 'whispers' floated about on Sunday 17 June and *excited me strangely*, Mary admitted. In this strange and momentous time, she explained what happened next: *Any stranger not in my secret would have considered that my conduct fully justified my partner Mr Day in sending me home . . . I never remember feeling more excited or more restless than upon that day and no sooner had night closed in upon us than, instead of making preparations for bed, this same stranger would have seen me wrap up – the nights were still cold – and start off for a long walk to Cathcart Hill, three and a half miles away. I stayed there until past midnight, but when I returned home, there was no rest for me, for I had found out that in the stillness of the night many regiments were marching down to the trenches, and that the dawn of day would be the signal that should let them loose upon the Russians. The few hours still left before daybreak were made the most of at Spring Hill.* Mary and her helpers prepared for the great onslaught by making cheese sandwiches, packing up fowls, tongues, ham, wine and spirits. She also filled a large bag with lint, bandages, needles, thread and medicines. At daybreak everything was loaded upon two mules and Mary led the way on horseback. Thus, her *little cavalcade* left the British Hotel before the sun of the fatal 18 June. At this early hour, the cavalry pickets had orders to stop anyone travelling to the scene of action. However, Mary was the sutler extraordinare and, even at this early hour, the men raised a shout for her. She tells us that she found Cathcart's Hill crowded with spectators. Carrying provisions to the troops, she learned that the attack upon the Redan had failed and very wisely went no further. But Mary's work was only just beginning for here she found plenty of officers who soon relieved her of her refreshments and some wounded men who found the contents of her bag useful. After this, she went to assist doctors at the temporary hospital where she was busy binding up wounds and tended to those who were badly injured. Throughout the day, Mary came under enemy fire with worrying regularity. Shot and shell whizzed about, but Mary was determined to reach those in need of her bandages and comforts. Dispensing human compassion at the risk of her life was rewarded with grateful words and smiles from broken men. Never satisfied, she pressed on to reach the casualties. It was here that, in throwing herself to the ground as a shell landed nearby, she fell heavily on her right thumb and dislocated it. The thumb never returned to its normal shape. With no water available, Mary washed her hands with sherry before she made her way back to Spring Hill, where she was told that her wayward lad who had accompanied her, *either frightened or tired of waiting*, had gone away with the mules. Where to? She mounted her horse, she went in search of the boy. When she found him, some three miles away, she admits to horse-whipping him, the *only satisfaction* she had. The tireless Mary moved on with bandages and refreshments and at *no little risk* to reach the wounded after the attack on General Eyre's Division.[82] It was a luckless day which left many dead. Indeed the long evening of 8 June was a sad one. Heart-rending news came in of those that had fallen. Mary was deeply upset because both the commanders who had fallen had been very good to her as the proprietor of the Hotel at Spring Hill. Among the other glorious dead was a Sir John C----- whom she remembered first meeting in her house in Jamaica.

On the following day, 19 June, Mary made her way to the battlefield with dread and anxiety *to see once more the faces of those who had been so kind to me in life*. The scene was a fearful sight and she prayed that she would never see its like again. But even as she prayed, she knew it was wishful thinking, because her usefulness in life was directly concerned with scenes of horror and distress. Nonetheless, it took a lot for her to be so horrified. Her distress was compounded when in the late afternoon the Russians handed over the bodies of her two senior officer friends. That moment was an indelible memory. She wrote: *They had stripped Sir John of epaulettes, sword and boots. Ah! how my heart felt for those at home who would soon hear of this day's fatal work! It was on the following day, I think, that I saw them bury him near Cathcart's Hill, where his tent had been pitched. If I had been in the least humour for what was ludicrous, the looks and curiosity of the Russians who saw me during the armistice would have afforded me considerable amusement. I wonder what rank they assigned me.* The terrors of war were not the only misfortunes that Mary Seacole had to endure. Cholera also raged around the camps, claiming victims from all ranks. Mary recalled with sorrow the death of a man she respected, a famous figure in the history of the Crimean War. As more generals died a *still greater calamity* happened. Lord Raglan, the *great soldier*, died. She had admired Raglan's iron courage, his kind words and gentle smile, which all added up to him being a good man. Mary Seacole knew Lord Raglan well enough and vouched for him being a caring commander. Of all the officers in the British Army, she regarded him as the most forthcoming, who took time to speak to the humblest of his men. Of his last days and following his death, she gives us the following insight: *During the time he was ill I was at headquarters several times, and once his servants allowed me to peep into the room where their master lay. I do not think they knew he was dying, but they seemed very sad and low – far more so than he for whom they feared. And on the day of his funeral I was there again. I never saw such heartfelt gloom as that which brooded on the faces of his attendants; but it was good to hear how they all, even the humblest had some kind memory of the great general whom Providence had called from his post at such a season of danger and distress. And once again they let me into the room in which the coffin lay, and I timidly stretched out my hand and touched a corner of the Union Jack which lay upon it; and then I watched it wind its way through the long lines of soldiery towards Kamiesch, while ever and anon, the guns thundered forth in sorrow, not in anger. And for days after, I could not help thinking of the 'Caradoc' which was ploughing its way through the sunny seas with its sad burden.* After these sad events, the mood among British soldiers began to return more or less to some semblance of its previous state. In her experience, as Mary put it was not usual for the British Army to *remain dull* and soon enough her British Hotel echoed with fun and laughter. We know a good deal about the horror and other aspects of the Crimean hostilities, but very little about the business side. How did she and Mr. Day run the British Hotel? We get clues from her autobiography. To begin with, the viability of the business warranted regular stock-taking. Several months later, the stores of the British Hotel were well filled, and significantly not only with every conceivable necessary of life, but with many of its most expensive luxuries. It was a high point in the Hotel's history and Mary had become the 'Mistress of Spring Hill' who could supply almost everything *on the spot, or obtained for you, if you had a little patience and did not mind a few weeks' delay.*[83]

But manage an establishment such as the British Hotel, Mary had, of necessity, to be responsive to changing conditions. Summertime, for example, brought its own plague of flies. Crimean flies were, in Mary's view, unlike any other, and such a visitation she hoped would not be repeated anywhere else. *Nature must surely have intended them for black-beetles*, she noted, and accidentally given them wings. They were a nuisance, hard to exterminate and difficult to escape their attentions either by night or by day. The flies spared no one; all suffered terribly. Mary relates the story of the Lieutenant, a 'close relative' of the Queen, serving in the Naval Brigade, who turned to her for help. *He evidently considered the fly nuisance the most trying portion of the Crimean campaign and far more consequence than the Russian shot and shell. 'Mami,' (he said he had been in the West Indies and so called me by the familiar term used by the Creole children) 'Mami, these flies respect nothing. Not content with eating my prog, they set to at night and make* a supper of me.' The evidence on his face showed traces of their attacks. 'Confound them, they'll kill me, Mami; they're every where, even in the trenches and you'd suppose they wouldn't care to go there from choice. What can you do for me, Mami?' There wasn't very much that Mary could do. But what little she could, she did for her Royal patient (who is now thought to have been Prince Victor of Hohenlohe-Langenburg, a half-nephew of Queen Victoria). If she was helpful to others, she was also creative and imaginative in her approach. On one occasion, she remembered riding to a store in Kadikoi, where she bought a piece of muslin which she made into a mosquito net for the Prince, who was delighted. When he fell ill later, Mary visited his quarters and gave him all the attention and care she was capable of. As the summer days passed, Mary learned from the guests at the British Hotel that more soldiers had joined the Russian Army which was preparing for a great battle. By August, the strong rumours became reality with the sound of guns and cannon. Thus the element of surprise was forestalled when at dawn on 16 August heavy firing was heard from the French positions by the Tchernaya River and both troops and spectators poured from all quarters in that direction. This call to battle found Mary *prepared and loaded*, and soon she was riding towards the scene of action and saw most of it. She witnessed the Russians as they made their way backwards and forwards across the river. She was near enough to see and hear the Russian officers cheer and wave their men forward *in the coolest, bravest manner, just before scores of them were shot down*. In the lull between the roar of the guns, she could hear excited cheers which at times signalled attack then repulse. Posterity was blessed by the fact that Mary was well placed to see what the Russians could not. She recalled that the squadrons of English and French cavalry waited *calmly yet impatiently* until the Russian's *partial success should bring their sabres into play*. Though unsentimental, this could not have been easy for Mary. What a resilient woman she was. And what depth of

Crimean War battle scene between Russian and Allied troops

understanding she showed in this violent man's world. The display of force was quite impressive and, as the Russians fell back, Mary painted a vivid picture of their retreat thus: *the dark-plumed Sardinians and red-pantalooned French spread out in pursuit and formed a picture so excitingly beautiful that we forgot the suffering and death they left behind.* At this stage, she had left her vantage point and went onto the field of battle where the carnage she witnessed was unbelievable even by her standards. Bodies lay strewn on the ground and the cries of pain filled the air. Water was the most precious want and getting it to the men who were still alive was an errand of mercy in which many officers and strangers engaged. But although the Russian guns were still firing, plunderers, especially the French, searched and stripped the dead of what was valuable, paying no regard to Mary's presence. Such hasty, even indecent behaviour did not meet her approval. True to character, her spirited complaints were met with laughter which she ignored. She was more charitable, patching up not only French and Sardinian soldiers, but also the Russian sick and wounded. Intrepid as ever, she proceeded to examine and try to help what was left of the shattered bodies before her. One Russian soldier was so badly wounded in the lower jaw as to put him beyond repair, she recalled. Yet she tried to dislodge a musket ball in his mouth. In a reflex action, he bit so hard as to leave a permanent scar on Mary's finger. Before this patient finally died, Mary recorded that his features had softened and a smile came over *his rough inexpressive face.*[84] No death left Mary unaffected and now she shifted her attention to another fallen Russian, an officer who was shot in the side. She watched him bear his pain with noble fortitude. As if to compensate for the wordless passing of his comrade, a second Russian, unable to speak English, was more demonstrative of his gratitude for her kindness.

Mary always had a ready, genuine smile for others and its value in the Crimea at this time was never greater. There were many to whom she gave her close attention, and it was fortunate that her warm, expressive, motherly face was the last that many soldiers saw. Giving, even for this pragmatic woman was, it seemed, better than receiving. Doing, being useful was its own reward! Mementoes, however, even relating to war, had their own value, all the more for Mary Seacole who was an 'actor' in the field of battle. While she found the idea of robbing either the living or the dead abhorrent, she could not resist snapping up a few souvenirs, a few buttons from the coats of dead soldiers.

Aftermath

Less than a month after the battle of the Tchernaya, Mary experienced her busiest and most eventful few weeks. Paradoxically, it was at a time when there was not much happening at Spring Hill. It was the calm before the big storm, the last bombardment of Sebastopol. Mary sets the scene. *Every one was either at his post, or too anxiously awaiting the issue of the last great bombardment to spend much time at the British Hotel. I think that I lost more of my patients and customers during those few weeks than during the whole previous progress of the siege. Scarce a night passed that I was not lulled to sleep with the heavy continuous roar of the artillery; scarce a morning dawned that did not usher in my day's work. The ear grew so accustomed during those weeks to the terrible roar that when Sebastopol fell the sudden quiet seemed unnatural and made us dull. And during the whole of this time the most perplexing rumours flew about, some having reference to the day of the assault, the majority relative to the last great effort which it was supposed the Russians would make to drive us into the sea. I confess these latter rumours now and then caused me temporary uneasiness, Spring Hill being on the direct line of route which actors in such a tragedy must take.* Mary spent a good deal of her time on Cathcart's Hill. Her 'curiosity and excitement' for war had not waned. In fact, it was aroused by the ongoing horrendous bombardment. She was anxious to get closer. Almost casually, at this juncture in her autobiography she wrote about the shells that fell now and then among the crowd of onlookers. Surprisingly, such danger did not disturb either Mary or the ghoulish visitors whose sense of excitement and expectation had far outweighed the danger of being killed. Such bravery as was shown by Mary and the spectators was, it seemed, matched by a ceremony that was held amidst the shelling. This was the moment chosen to honour a select few with the Order of the Bath. For Mary, who was always on the go, this was a time to stop, a moment of which she was proud to bear witness. As she put it, *although it cost me a day, I considered that I had fairly earned the pleasure*. She felt a sense of deep personal satisfaction and for the occasion she baked a cake which was dressed up with bright banners and flags. Mary acknowledges that she *received great kindness from the officials at the ceremony, and from the officers . . . who recognised me*. A few days after the ceremony, the ongoing bombardment had become so fearful that Mary thought the end of the world was at hand. The city was pounded with, it seemed, every shot and shell. She gave this account of what happened next during this action: *The firing began at early dawn . . . sleep was impossible; so I arose and set out for my old station on Cathcart's Hill. And here with refreshments for the anxious lookers on, I spent most of my time, right glad of any excuse to witness the last scene of the siege. It was from this spot that I saw fire after fire break out in Sebastopol and watched all night the beautiful yet terrible effect of a great ship blazing in the harbour and lighting up the adjoining country for miles.* On the morning of 8 September the capricious Crimean weather changed again: it became cold and wintry. And as she had done on the terrible 18 June, Mary anticipated a catastrophe. Early that morning, she was already on her horse laden with necessary supplies. Once again she encountered sentries who were posted to deter onlookers from progressing further. Her reputation had, however, preceded her and now it served as her passport as the officers relaxed the rule in her favour. Having made this journey so often, Mary found herself once more at an early hour in her familiar spot with her tried and tested medicines, bandages and drinks for the wounded and fatigued. What she did not expect was that the disastrous consequences of the day would so closely approximate the losses of the last attack. After the incessant din of the morning's battle, suddenly at midday the cannonade ceased and from her vantage point Mary saw an almost unbelievable sight. The Malakhoff Redoubt had been taken by the French, but the British assault on the Redan had failed. She proceeded to attend to the

William Simpson's lithograph of the Malakhoff Hill after its capture by French troops on the 8 September 1855

large numbers of wounded, among whom were many officers of her beloved 97th Regiment, whom she had known in Jamaica. Their losses were terrible. Engrossed in her care of the wounded, she was careless of her own safety as shells fell here and there. Luckily, she escaped injury when a shell fell so close as to make her *seriously frightened*. Nonetheless, she took home a fragment of the shell as a souvenir. Despite this brush with injury or even death, Mary was a conspicuous figure on the battlefield, applying herself with selfless diligence. At this awful time, Mary was spotted by *The Times* correspondent William Howard Russell, whom she had often spotted *taking down notes and sketches of the scene, under fire.*[85]

Mary had seen Russell many times before, but this was the occasion when the keen-eyed correspondent made her a household name. He was the first war correspondent and his reports from the Crimea were hugely influential with the British public. If Mary Seacole was little known in England hitherto, now Russell was ready to lift her from obscurity and put her centre stage, by informing the readers of *The Times*: 'I have seen her go down under fire with her little store of creature comforts for our wounded men; and a more tender and skilful hand about a wound or broken limb could not be found among our best surgeons I saw her at the assault on the Redan, at the Tchernaya, at the fall of Sebastopol, laden not with plunder, good old soul, but with wine, bandages and food for the wounded or the prisoners.'[86]

Mary laboured among the fallen men all day and stayed on Cathcart's Hill late into the night. She watched awe-struck as Sebastopol burned. The chill wind made her shiver as she approached Spring Hill. She had a sleepless night which was lit-up by the glare of the burning city. Mary believed that, unlike herself, the weary soldiers slept

Known as 'the first and greatest of War Correspondents,' William Howard Russell was born in Dublin on 28 March 1820. His journalistic career before 1854 was relatively undistinguished, but his great opportunity came when J T Delane, editor of *The Times*, sent him out to cover the impeding war with Russia. His reports on the suffering of the troops in the Crimea provoked the public outcry that resulted in Florence Nightingale being sent to Scutari. After the war, he was the most famous journalist in Britain, covering the Indian Mutiny and founding the *Army and Navy Gazette* in 1859. He was knighted in 1895. He died on 10 February 1907.

soundly even through the terrible night of the final assault. In fact, for those who could and did sleep, they woke up to find Sebastopol deserted, 'a heap of ruins to its victors,' and before noon on the following day none but dead and dying Russians were in the south side of the once famous and beautiful city.

At last, there was the good news that the Russians were to evacuate Sebastopol. This had the effect of dispelling most of the tiredness of the previous days. For Mary's part, there was a challenge to be met. She offered bets that she would be the first woman from the English lines to enter the fallen city. Although she needed an official pass to enter, when she did so, predictably she was carrying refreshments. Once more her reputation and her good works got her through. But as she passed the sentries, those officers who had not been given passes did not hide their annoyance at being thwarted from entering Sebastopol. Mary recalled riding through the city, many parts of which were still ablaze. Explosions here and there added to the dangers. Nonetheless, curiosity and excitement drove her on. She stopped often to attend to officers and men in need of refreshments and attention. A few had acquainted themselves with Russian wine cellars and were *ingloriously drunk* when Mary reached them. This was an attractive option for the vanquished also who were faced with the choice of memory and forgetting. Here too, Mary was offered, and took, many trophies, including *a gaily decorated altar-candle studded with gold and silver stars, an old cracked China teapot, a cracked bell and a parasol*. Whilst collecting these items, she never forgot that she was in the fearful city that had caused so much death and suffering. As she passed along the streets, amid many hazards, she was increasingly aware of being exposed to Russian fire. In spite of their watchfulness, some in her entourage had narrowly escaped being hit. Further into the city, the dangers were more apparent as fires broke out all around her, while mines exploded without warning. With great difficulty, Mary and her

A pontoon bridge enabled the Russians to abandon the burning Sebastopol for the safety of their northern forts

companions succeeded in getting into the part of Sebastopol held by the French. Here, she nearly got into serious trouble. While inspecting the ruins and observing some Frenchmen plundering a house, she was accused by a young American sailor of being a Russian spy. Predictably, she was incensed by the audacious charge and refused to dismount her horse. Instead, she hit the first soldier who tried to lay hands on her with the bell (a souvenir), which made the Frenchmen more determined to arrest Mary. They attempted to manhandle her into the guard house. Mary resisted and screamed for help. Just then, a French officer whom she had treated as a patient at Spring Hill after the battle of the Tchernaya, appeared and wasted no time in ordering Mary's release. But this was not quite the end of the matter for immediately after, Mary (now 51 years old) flew at the American who had caused the trouble. She used her bell and her companions wielded their riding whips to inflict what she felt was just punishment.

After the French soldiers' apologies to Mary, she acquired another 'trophy' of incalculable value while on the way back to Spring Hill. It was a picture of the Madonna some 8–10 feet in length which had been cut from above the altar of some church in Sebastopol. Mary was not very religious, but she was appreciative of those who were believers. Fundamentally, she was a passionate humanitarian, a doer, rather than a preacher/spectator. Nonetheless, she was appreciative of the image she had brought home. *I am no judge of such things,* she reflected, *but I think, although the painting is rather coarse, that the face of the Virgin and the heads of the cherubim that fill the cloud from which she is descending are soft and beautiful. There is a look of divine calmness and heavenly love in the Madonna's face which is very striking; and, perhaps during the long and awful siege many a knee was bent in worship before it, and many a heart found comfort in its soft loving gaze.* The next day Mary went back to Sebastopol, where her exploration led her to yet more of the city's horrors. Suffice it to say here that she found there a *woeful hospital* where thousands of dead and dying had been left by the retreating Russians, which was *enough to unnerve the strongest and sicken the most experienced.*[87] Even for her, this was perhaps the most harrowing sight she had ever seen. Thereafter, the dutiful Mrs Seacole also returned to the Redan, where at every turn there was still danger. She noted the 'houses' opened by some French women in Sebastopol, but she was not tempted to do the same. She was content to see through the Crimean campaign from her war-seasoned old quarters at Spring Hill.

At last, the Crimean campaign was over and the 'great work,' as Mary called it, was accomplished. The Russians had retired, and a *novel position* existed. The questions Mary and others then posed were: What was to be done? Was there to be more fighting? The answers to such questions were, of course, in the hands of the strategists at the British Headquarters and their leaders at home.

While deliberations continued, the soldiers diverted their attention to amusements with *the same energy and activity {that} made Sebastopol a heap of ruins and a well-filled cemetery.* Now they were *set to work as eager to kill their present enemy, time, as they had lately been to destroy their fled enemies the Russians.* The fear and terror of the battle for Sebastopol in the summer was followed by what in Mary's words was a beautiful autumn which preceded the second winter of the Crimean campaign. The survivors felt they had earned the right to some relaxation and enjoyment.

In the aftermath of the Crimean War, the terrible events needed to be recorded for posterity. William Howard Russell was rightly regarded as the first war correspondent, and Roger Fenton was the first British war photographer because of his work in the Crimea, but the title of the first war photographer must go to Karol de Szathmari. William Simpson became the celebrated

The photographer Roger Fenton arrived at Balaclava in March 1855, commissioned by the print-seller Thomas Agnew to make photographic studies of the campaign in the Crimea, making him the first British photographer to work in a war zone. Born in 1819, he had originally trained as an artist, but took up the new medium of photography between 1848 and 1851. He rapidly rose to prominence in his new field, coming to the attention of the Royal Family, which greatly enhanced his status. After the Crimean War, he continued as a photographer until suddenly abandoning his work in 1862. He died in 1869.

British artist of the Crimean War, and writers, such as Tolstoy, Tennyson and Dickens have made reference to the War.

How much more could those who survived the war take?

Not surprisingly, the pendulum of human endurance had now swung the other way as a carnival spirit infected the visitors, officers and men. Life was short and pleasure was not an option for too long. But now, it was hunted keenly. It was to be had in sports, pastimes, theatricals, parties and, of course, dinners. Mary's dinner parties included men of high rank, such as the Duc de Rouchefoucault, a Prince of the French Imperial family, and Viscount Talon. Many attested to the quality of her cooking.[88]

It was clear that now, after the fall of Sebastopol, Mary was more amenable to the French and in doing her best for them, she learned a great deal. Her verdict on them was this *It is true that they carried from Sebastopol the lion's share of glory! My belief is that they deserved it, having borne by far a larger proportion of suffering.* While Mary basked in the high praise she received for her dinners at Spring Hill, one wonders whether she, in turn, complimented her unsung, devoted black cook and other helpers? Understandably, she was the one to whom attention was directed. Toasts were drunk to her good health. The French Prince Talon paid several visits to the British Hotel. She revelled in the activities of the higher classes. At this time, and in such grand company, Mary spoke of hunting in the Crimea and said that her experiences of attending Crimean (horse) races were perfect. The 'Sport of Kings,' held just before Christmas, was an event of great interest, which

The pioneer war artist William Simpson was born in Glasgow in 1823. After training as a lithographer, he worked for various lithography companies until 1854, when he became a war artist. He went out to Balaclava in November 1854 to make sketches on the spot. His drawings were shown to Lord Raglan who passed them on to the Queen. After the fall of Sebastopol, 80 of Simpson's Crimean drawings were lithographed and he had an audience with the Queen. In 1866, he became a special artist for the *Illustrated London News*, where he worked for 25 years. He died on 17 August 1899 in Willesden, London.

Mary attended and was better prepared with each meeting. She was struck by how well the managers of these Crimean races replicated the old familiar scenes at home. Things had improved markedly after the earlier shortages and mismanagement in the camps. Communications with England were far better now than they had been when Mary first arrived in the Crimea. A reflection of this was to be seen in the high quality of racing gear: the racing saddles, boots, silk caps and jackets. And incredibly, as if anticipating the well-known African tipster and showman of the 1960s, Prince Monololu, Mary observed that *some soldiers blackened their faces and came out as Ethiopian serenaders admirably, although it would puzzle the most ingenious to guess where they got their wigs and banjos from.* How odd that in the scene of such fear and the terror of battles past and foreboding of those to come that there should be this show of normal life. A few weeks before Christmas, there was a great explosion in the French ammunition dump, in which many were killed. This resulted in friction between French and British soldiers over the two armies' relative performances at the Malakhoff and the Redan respectively. There was also at this time a rare occurrence: Mary fell ill, for the first and only time in the Crimea. Considering her proximity to sickness and disease, from Cruces to the Crimea, one is struck by the extraordinary physical and mental constitution she possessed. Nonetheless, her illness, *not of much consequence*, she attributed to a sudden cold snap that had taken her by surprise. During this lapse in health, apart from the kindness of her soldier friends, she also received *much sympathy and many presents of warm clothing, etc.; but the most delicate piece of attention was shown me by one of the Sappers and Miners who, hearing the report that I was dead, positively came down to Spring Hill to take my measure for a coffin.* Rather than be offended, Mary felt flattered, touched by such *thoughtful attention.* Could she ever have too much attention? So when Christmas eventually came, it was with pleasant memories of home and 'home comforts.' Mary was also cheered by news from abroad which reflected her growing reputation in the Crimea. One of her greetings read: 'A merry Christmas . . . and many of them. Although you will not write to us, we see your name frequently in the newspapers, from which we judge that you are strong and hearty. All your old Jamaican friends are delighted to hear of you, and say that you are an honour to the Isle of Springs.' Mary's pro-British stance had served her well and now at Christmas she did the English thing as hostess of the British Hotel. She planned to serve plum pudding and mince pies. It was a Christmas which she hoped her 'sons' would never forget, and for three weeks before, she wrote, *my time was fully occupied in making preparations for it.* The thought that this could well be the soldiers last Christmas gave the occasion added significance. While it meant hard work for the great organiser/proprietor of the British Hotel, it was a magnet for Britons who eagerly anticipated her wholesome and exotic cooking. Mary rose to the task and her Christmas fare was a huge success, so much so that one customer referring to an order for mince pies for a certain Captain said: *sure, he likes them well done, Ma'am. Bake 'em as brown as your own purty face, darlint.* This last reference to her colour did not escape Mary's attention, hence its inclusion in her autobiography. After many hours of preparation and cooking, all that Mary had intended to offer her customers and friends was served up and all were duly satisfied by her Herculean efforts. But what about her own Christmas Dinner? Rules were rules and as Mary said, she had to wait until 8pm before she could sit down to dinner. Then New Year's Day brought its own demands for pies and puddings and reminded Mary's patients of the home comforts for which they longed. One patient in particular had caught Mary's attention and left an indelible impression. He had been *a most industrious and honest fellow,* whom Mary found *very weak and ill.* She stayed with him for quite a while and noted that before she left him, *kind fancy had brought to his bedside his wife and children from his village home in England, and I could hear him talking to them in a low and joyful tone. Poor, poor fellow! The New Year so full of hope and happiness had dawned upon him, but he did not live to see the wild flowers spring up peacefully through the war-trodden sod before Sebastopol.*[89] So ended that memorable Christmas/New Year celebrations at the British Hotel.

With the first days of the New Year, the prospects of reaching a peaceful settlement and of going home were uppermost in the minds of the officers, soldiers and, to Mary, even though the consequences, as we shall see were unfavourable to her. Everyone had had enough and waited for news of the cessation of hostilities, which was not long in coming. Before the Armistice was signed, Mary noted there were instances of closer relations, *advances of friendship* between the Russians and their adversaries. Thus foes became friends and the banks of the Tchernaya were the scene of a strange camaraderie. Mounted on her horse, Mary, who was among the first to visit Tchernaya, wrote how *very delighted the Russians were to see an English woman,* another indication of how strongly she identified with Britishness that she had no idea of being Jamaican, which was a British colony anyway. She went on to say: *I wonder if they* [the Russians] *thought that they* [the English] *all had my complexion.* The colour of her skin had not deterred her before and it was not going to do so now. She soon fell in with the *current amusement* of swapping coins with the Russians. After this interlude of exchange and camaraderie came the last shots of any consequence. It signalled the final moments of hostilities and ushered in the good news of peace. Soon after, Mary wrote, the home-going was accompanied *with happy faces and light hearts, and some kind thoughts and warm tears for the comrades left behind.* Ironically, since war was profitable, while Mary was 'very glad' to hear of peace, it came at a price. As she rightly felt, everyone who had used her Hotel was aware that it would cause her 'ruin.' The Crimean War and the British Hotel were inseparable, both conceptually and practically. The magnitude of what she now faced was recalled in her autobiography: *We had lately made extensive additions to our store and outhouses – our shelves were filled with articles laid in at a great cost, and which were now unsaleable, and which it would be equally impossible to carry home. Everything from our stud of horses and mules down to our latest consignments from home, must be sold for any price! And, as it happened for many things worth a year ago their weight in gold, no purchaser could now be found.* In fact, not long after the war, the firm of Seacole and Day would be declared bankrupt. Depressing as her thoughts about her business prospects were, before leaving the Crimea, Mary decided to see more of the hinterland. In Baktchiserai, she had an amusing and pleasant time, even though her hungry companions had to forego food in a hamper in which they discovered a rat! The last peaceful days of winter gave way to spring, and the scene of the troops' orderly departure was touchingly recorded by Mary Seacole: *As they passed the Iron House* [the British Hotel] *where so much of life's action had been compressed into so short a space of time – they would stop and give us a parting cheer, while very often the kind-hearted officers would find time to run into the British Hotel to bid us good-bye, and give us a farewell shake of the hand; for you see war, like death, is a great leveller and mutual suffering and endurance had made us all friends.* Wise words from a veteran. From this time of parting, Mary had kept many a letter and scribblings, one of which read: *My dear Mrs Seacole and my dear Mr Day, I have called here four times this day, to wish you good bye. I am so sorry I was not fortunate enough to see you. I shall still hope to see you tomorrow morning. We march at seven a.m.* Despite her apparent composure at this time, the to-ing and fro-ing of departure from the Crimea all seemed *strange and somewhat sad* to Mrs Seacole. In a revealing and quite understandable passage she wrote: *sometimes I felt that I could not sympathise with the glad faces and happy hearts of those who were looking forward to the delights of home, and the joy of seeing once more the old familiar faces remembered so fondly in the fearful trenches and the hard-fought battlefields. Now and then we would see a lounger with a blank face, taking no interest in the bustle of departure, and with him I acknowledged to have more fellow-feeling than with the others, for he, as well as I, clearly had no home to go to! He was soldier by choice and necessity, as well as by profession. He had no home, no loved friends; the peace would bring no particular pleasure to him, whereas war and action were necessary to his existence, gave him excitement, occupation, the chance of promotion. Now and then, but seldom, however, you come across such a disappointed one. Was it not so with me? Had I not been happy through the months of toil and danger, never knowing what fear or depression was, finding every moment of the day mortgaged hours in advance, and earning sound sleep and contentment by sheer hard work? What better or happier lot could possibly befall me? And, alas! How likely was it that my present occupation gone, I might long in vain for another so stirring and so useful!! Besides which, it was pretty sure that I should go to England poorer than I left it, and although I was not ashamed of poverty; beginning life again in the autumn – I mean late in the summer of life – is hard up-hill work.*

Then came the moment of her own Crimean farewell. She left with many testimonials to her devoted work in the Crimea and distinguished between those she received from officers and those from the enlisted men. She preferred the thoughts and letters from members of the latter group and inserted one written on 16 June 1856 in her autobiography: *MY DEAR MRS. SEACOLE – As you are about to leave the Crimea, I avail myself of the only opportunity which may occur for some time, to acknowledge my gratitude to you, and to thank you for the kindness which I, in common with many others, received at your hands, when attacked with cholera in the spring of 1855. But I have no language to do it suitably.*

I am truly sensible that your kindness far exceeded my claims upon my sympathy. It is said by some of your friends, I hope truly, that you are going to England. There can be none from the Crimea more welcome there, for your kindness in the sick-tent, and your heroism in the battle-field, have endeared you to the whole army.

I am sure when her most gracious Majesty the Queen shall have become acquainted with the service you have gratuitously rendered to so many of her brave soldiers, her generous heart will thank you. For you have been an instrument in the hands of the Almighty to preserve many a gallant heart to the empire, to fight and win her battles, if ever again war may become a necessity. Please to accept this from your most grateful humble servant. W.J.TYNAN.[90]

Last Years Crimean Heroine

Mary arrived back in England in August 1856. A few days later, she attended a public banquet in Kennington. The occasion was to honour those who served in the Crimea. It was a huge celebration attended by 2,000 troops that packed into the Royal Surrey Gardens.[91] A *News of the World* reporter wrote: 'Immediately behind the chair in front of the orchestra was a very handsome trophy of flags and laurel wreaths, with Redan and Malakhoff inscribed on each side and Miss Nightingale's name in the centre . . . among the fair visitors in the upper side of the gallery [i.e. where the uninvited quests sat] was Mrs Seacole, whose dark features were quite radiant with delight and good humour as she gazed on the pleasant scene below.'[92]

The Times, on the other hand, stated that amidst '. . . the illustrious [onlookers] was Mrs Seacole, whose appearance awakened the most rapturous enthusiasm. The soldiers not only cheered her, but chaired her around the gardens, and she really might have suffered from the oppressive attentions of her admirers, were it not that two sergeants of extraordinary stature gallantly undertook to protect her from the pressure of the crowd.'[93]

Portrait of Mary Seacole by William Simpson

While Mary was being uproariously acclaimed in public, Florence Nightingale, that other Crimean heroine, opted for seclusion.[94] Put simply, Mary loved publicity and thrived on it, while Florence did not. After this event, Mary returned to Aldershot where she was staying, but by October, she was in London, where she lived at 1 Tavistock Street near Drury Lane and Covent Garden. In her rented room she lived modestly. Money was in short supply, but there was an abundance of well-wishers and friends from whom she received a good deal of moral support during this period when the Day and Seacole business was bankrupt. Eventually, when a settlement was reached in court, the Judge awarded both Day and Seacole an allowance of two guineas each.[95]

Two weeks later, a letter was published in *The Times* reminding readers of Mary's sterling service in the Crimea and the importance of 'acts of benevolence' at this time of need. The writer proposed a donation of £20 and asked others to join him. Further correspondence resulted in pledges of money and *Punch* chimed in:

'Dame Seacole was a kindly old soul,
And a kindly old soul was she:
You might call for your pot, you might call for your pipe,
In her tent on the "Col" so free . . .

And now the good soul is "in the hole",
What redcoat in all the land,
But to set her on her legs again,
Will not lend a willing hand.'[96]

Early in the New Year, the firm of Seacole and Day was legally free to operate again and Mary felt a new lease of life. But thoughts of the war were never far from her mind. All the moreso because she was never formally awarded any of the Crimean campaign medals that she wore during the earlier court hearings. Given that there is no record that she ever received an award, according to biographer Jane Robinson 'It is more than likely that Mary "distinguished" herself. Miniatures were obtained by her army friends, or bought on the open market, and . . . she resolved to wear them, by right to commemorate the fallen and in recognition of her commitment to the British cause. Miniatures are not real medals: they're items of jewellery. But what they signified to Mary went far beyond vain ornament.'[97]

At the time, many eye-witness accounts of the Crimean War were being published and the publisher James Blackwood commissioned Mary to write her memoirs, *Wonderful Adventures of Mrs Seacole in Many Lands*. The book was helped by William Howard Russell's endorsement which appears at the beginning, addressed: 'TO THE READER: I should have thought that no preface would have been required to introduce Mrs Seacole to the British public, or to recommend a book which must, from the circumstances in which the subject of it was placed, be unique in literature. If singleness of heart, true clarity and Christian works; if trials and sufferings, dangers and perils, encountered boldly by a helpless woman on her errand of mercy in the camp and in the battlefield, can excite sympathy or move curiosity, Mary Seacole will have many friends and many readers. She is no Anna Comnena, who presents us with a verbose history, but a plain truth speaking woman who had lived an adventurous life amid scenes which have never yet found a historian among the actors on the stage where they passed. I have witnessed her devotion and courage; I have already borne testimony to her services to all who needed them. She is the first who has redeemed the name 'Sutler' from the suspicion of worthlessness, mercenary baseness and

WONDERFUL ADVENTURES

of

M^{RS} SEACOLE

LONDON

JAMES BLACKWOOD

PATERNOSTER ROW

plunder; and I trust that England will not forget one who nursed her sick, who sought out her wounded to aid and succour them, and who performed the last offices for some of her illustrious dead.'[98]

In the meantime, her circumstances had not improved and were becoming increasingly, embarrassingly evident. She urgently needed money and fortunately a subscription fund was officially set up and a committee of trustees was established. To achieve their objective, a series of fund-raising concerts to be held in the Royal Surrey Gardens was planned. Finally in July 1857, Mary's *Wonderful Adventures* was published. A recent account, describes *Wonderful Adventures* as 'part autobiography, part travelogue, not to raise the profile of Afro-Caribbeans or women, but of [Mary] herself. It is neither a political statement nor an artistic exercise; it's a glorious advertisement, written by a celebrity fully in control of her own image. What disturbs many modern readers most about the book is Mary's refusal to identify more fully with her African heritage.'[99] Nonetheless, the book was successful. Within eight months, the first print run was sold and it was reissued in March 1858. What perhaps prevented the book from enjoying even greater success was the fact that just prior to its publication, the Indian Mutiny flared up and news reached London of the massacre of Britons in Meerut, India. The savagery of the dark-skinned mutineers cause revulsion among the white British populace and may have affected the sales of her book. Nonetheless, *Wonderful Adventures* did Mary Seacole proud and the Surrey Gardens concerts drew large crowds. But Mary only received £57, which was nowhere near enough assistance.

Sometime between 1859–60 Mary returned to Jamaica, and soon after she heard of the death of her friend and fellow-cook, Alexis Soyer. While she was on the island a political demonstration in Morant Bay resulted in the local militia

A mob storm the Court House in Morant Bay, St Thomas-in-the-East, Jamaica

firing at the crowd killing 28 people. The British public was shocked by the order given by Governor Edward Eyre, who was recalled to London. Thereafter, Jamaica's Assembly was replaced by Crown Colony government. Subsequently Mary became a direct beneficiary of this liberal approach and the Seacole Fund was re-established in London in 1867. With donations coming in from high profile individuals and royalty, including the Queen, Mary's financial position improved.

By 1870, now in her 65th year, she looked suitably venerable and was highly regarded by cross-section of British society. Not surprisingly, with the outbreak of the Franco-Prussian war, Mary was ready once more with her medicine kit to travel to the aid of soldiers in need. She duly applied to be of service, but was not allowed to go because officials felt she was too much of a national asset to lose. Her disappointment can only be imagined. However, what has survived from that time is a letter from Florence Nightingale to Sir Harry Verney dated 5 August 1870 and marked 'Burn':

'Mrs Seacole
I dare say you know more about her than I do.

She kept – I will not call it a "bad house" but something not very unlike it – in the Crimean War.

She was very kind to the men & what is more, to the Officers – & did some good – & made many drunk.

(A shameful ignorant imposture was practised on the Queen who subscribed to the "Seacole Testimonial.")

I had the greatest difficulty in repelling Mrs Seacole's advances, & in preventing association between her & my nurses (absolutely out of the question) when we established 2 hospitals nursed by us between Kadikoi & the "Seacole Establishment" in the Crimea. But I was successful. Without any open collision with Mrs Seacole – which I was

Edward John Eyre was born in Bedfordshire in 5 August 1815. He settled in Australia and became a famous explorer, winning the Royal Geographical Society's Gold Medal for a 1,000-mile trek through north and west Australia. He was appointed to a number of colonial governorships in New Zealand and later the West Indies, but his awkward personality and low opinion of blacks caused problems. He was acting as Lieutenant-Governor of Jamaica when the Morant Bay rebellion of 1865 broke out, and his draconian response lead to his recall. It was the end of his career and he died in 1901.

anxious to avoid – (You will understand that any "rivalry" between the "Seacole" & the "Nightingale" "Establishments" was very much to be averted.)

Anyone who employs Mrs Seacole will introduce much kindness – also much drunkenness & improper conduct, wherever she is.

She had then, however, one or more "persons" with her, whom (I conclude) she has not now. I conclude (& believe) that respectable Officers were entirely ignorant of what I . . . could not help knowing, as a Matron & Chaperone & Mother of the Army.'[100]

If this harsh judgement hints at more than a whiff of jealousy, there was more to come from the revered Lady with the Lamp who, unlike Mary, was granted an audience with the Queen. Why? Florence was the British Establishment's own home-grown Crimean heroine. Mary was a colonial and, in spite of her fame, she was perceived by many as being very unusual, un-English in her bearing and manner and therefore on the periphery of the British public's consciousness. Florence, in spite of the revered place she held in the heart of the nation, was nevertheless jealous of Mary's celebrity. She was determined to push Mary out of the limelight, and worse, even to besmirch her reputation. A recent article in *History Today*, cites a number of reasons why Mary was never invited to meet Queen Victoria, including the charges contained in the above-mentioned letter that Mary had served alcohol to officers and men, that she pleaded poverty when she shouldn't and, scandalously, that she had an illegitimate daughter named Sally, a relative who, like everyone else, called Mary 'Mother.'[101]

On this controversial matter of Sally being Mary's illegitimate child, Florence Nightingale pointed the finger of suspicion at a Mr Henry Bunbury as being the father.[102] This may not be true, for no evidence has been produced to support it. But the question of Sally's paternity is an intriguing one. Given that in her autobiography Mary had been economical with the truth about her early life in Jamaica, if Sally was Mary's daughter it is more than likely that her father would have been someone whom Mary knew well and trusted. She mentions such a person often in her story, someone with whom she had the closest and longest association. And judging from her tone of voice, Mary respected this person more than any other. The man I refer to is Mr Thomas Day, an Englishman whom Mary had met in Jamaica. He may well have known Mary at the time of her marriage to Edwin Seacole, who was interestingly, throughout the marriage, in very poor health. The business, a store, that Mary and Edwin had set up in Black River had to be abandoned and, as mentioned earlier, soon after their return to Kingston, Edwin died. As far as we know, the Seacoles had no children. Nonetheless, Mary's association with Mr Day seemed to have become closer for they were both attracted to business ventures, as was Edwin. But, unlike the sickly Edwin, Mr Day was a robust entrepreneur. We first hear of Mr Day in Mary's autobiography where she states that he had invited her to Navy Bay. *He was a distant connection of my late husband*, she wrote, *a man who treated me with great kindness.*[103]

Researchers have explained that Mary had left Jamaica for Central America because of the many proposals of marriage she had been receiving. But she withstood all their attentions, saying she was confident enough to remain an unprotected female and as she herself put it many years later *I do not mind confessing* [that] *one of the hardest struggles of my life in Kingston was to resist the pressing candidates for the late Mr Seacole's shoes.*[104] But while marriage was out of the question, it does not mean that she was against a relationship. Fully in control of how she remembers and writes her story, Mary places Mr Day in Escribanos (Navy Bay), Central America where they met, thus dispelling the argument that she was escaping the attentions of the opposite sex. Mr Day was there on business relating to mines and gold-prospecting. Interestingly, before she went to meet Mr Day she had already heard about the conflict in the Crimea and Britain's growing interest and involvement. In fact, war seemed inevitable and when she and Mr Day met in Escribanos, they may well have discussed the subject of Mary's ambition of going to the war zone to help her wounded 'sons', and to this end, she travelled to England to offer herself for recruitment as a nurse in the Crimea.

After she had failed to be taken on as a nurse in London, she again met Mr Day. Was it the chance meeting that Mary makes it out to be? Or did they plan to meet there? In her autobiography, she says that while her *new scheme* [namely, opening a hotel for invalids] *was maturing*[105] and after meeting Mr Day, she decided to pay her way to the Crimea. But, she speculated: *My funds, although they might carefully husbanded, carry me over the three thousand miles and land me in Balaclava, would not support me there long.*[106] How much more than her passage money did she have? Did her friend Mr Day help? It is more than likely that he did, because as Mary tells us, he too was heading in the same direction, to Balaclava on shipping business, which would have been music to Mary's ears. So far, a pattern begins to emerge in their relationship and one is tempted to ask: were their meetings fortuitous or planned? Now, from London, she was ready to follow Mr Day on to Balaclava where she anticipated his letters.

Eventually, on Mary's arrival in the Crimea, she and Mr Day as 'partners' engaged in an incredible undertaking of establishing their Seacole and Day British Hotel. It was an historic coming-together of Mary and her friend on a project that would catapult Mary to public prominence; and to get it off the ground, a large capital outlay was needed. How much money did Mary have at this time? We have no answer to this question. All she admits to is that the Hotel cost 'no less' than £800. Was this an underestimate? From here on, Mr Day was always around, close to hand, supervising and giving Mary advice even about her own safety. Judging from her autobiography, Mr Day was Mary's silent, but crucially close partner, which should not detract from the fact that she was indeed the colourful lady ambassador, the one who brought the enterprise alive.

Then, as the war raged on about them, Sally shows up at the British Hotel and gossip and comments came from visitors such as Alexis Soyer and Florence Nightingale came to visit. Both were astonished to see the handsome teenage girl with brown skin and blue eyes. Florence thought she was the daughter of a Mr Bunbury. If Sally was 14, then her birth in Jamaica would have been sometime around 1841 when both Mary and Mr Day were in Jamaica. Mary tells us that Sally was not her daughter. Nonetheless, her relationship with Mr Day remained paramount, for finally at the end of the bloody war, they consoled each other over their losses, not only in stock, but also their British Hotel. On their return to England Mary and Mr Day were together again in Aldershot, where together they faced bankruptcy until they were both adjudged legally free to practice in business once more. Although Mary has been economical with personal details of her early and later life, it is clear that Mr Day played a key role in helping her to realise her visionary Crimean scheme. She knew him well enough before and after her husband's death and then into her old age, but although the Crimean heroine has provided us with the clues, no one has hitherto recognised or detailed Mary Seacole's close, crucial and enduring relationship with Mr Day.

Given that Victorian Britain was securely founded upon a combination of race, class and colour, it was incredible that Mary got as far as she did. This, in large part, also also help to explain why Florence Nightingale was allowed to reign supreme. Even at the height of Mary's fame, although the British press had praised Mary in the post-war euphoria, they paid respect where it was due, but nothing more. And when the Crimean troops of all ranks who knew and loved Mary had passed away, her reputation among the living seemed to have died too. Fortunately, she enjoyed a

A marble bust of Mary Seacole by Gliechen

wide circle of friends and proudly wore her 'medals'. By 1876, at the age of 71, she was living free of debt, much more easily at 26 Upper George Street Portman Square. It was time for her to make her will and five years later she changed address again to 3 Cambridge Street. For this intrepid traveller, it was to be her last move. She died in May 1881 and left an estate work £2,615. 11s. 7d, a huge sum at the time.[107]

Mary was buried in St Mary's Roman Catholic Cemetery in Kensal Green and was quickly forgotten. Then, 67 years after her death, a shipload of Jamaicans arrived aboard the appropriately named SS *Empire Windrush*, heralding an influx of Commonwealth migrants, including a number of qualified and trainee nurses. Although Mary Seacole was the 19th-century precursor of these 20th-century Caribbean nurses, few, if any, of them knew who she was. With continued migration and settlement, the children of the Empire and their descendants in the post-1950 era, engaged in struggles of race, class and colour in Britain and began to assert their identities and claim their heritage. There was a thirst for knowledge and researchers abounded. Thus history and culture came into play and answers to the migrants' questions revealed the hidden histories of heroic figures including Mary Seacole. In 1973, her memory was restored, with a ceremony at her graveside; and in 2004, she was voted the 'Greatest Black Briton.' So, 148 years later, in post-colonial Britain, Mary Seacole's reputation is greater than it was in 1856. Tirelessly remedying ills on three continents, she was truly international, a one-off, ahead of her time. In recognition of her heroic struggles, the Jamaican Government had in 1990 awarded their Order of Merit to her. And, as if in recognition of these developments, a long-lost portrait of her, an oil painting by Albert Charles Challen was recently found.

Mary Seacole by Albert Charles Challen

Whether or not she was the greatest Black Briton, few could doubt the happiness and pride with which she demonstrated her Britishness. But while the particularity of her 'blackness' is important, it was her enduring goodness of heart that is the hallmark of her greatness. As an individual, she fought prejudice (some argue she could have done more) and treated it with the contempt it deserved. It was her way of confronting racism, of trying to humanise negative 'Britishness,' which to a degree she had achieved when she won hearts and minds and became 'Mother of the British Army.' Today, the 'lost' painting of Mary Seacole in profile is proudly displayed at the National Portrait Gallery which, ironically was the former site of the barracks from which the troops bound for the Crimea had left in 1854. This image captures the enigma that is Mary Seacole, a powerful evocation of the care-worn but determined face of a matronly, self-possessed humanitarian.

Notes

1. Mary Seacole, *Wonderful Adventures of Mrs. Seacole in Many Lands* (James Blackwood, London: 1858) p 1, hereafter Adventures.
2. Rex Nettleford, 'Freedom of Thought and Experience: Nineteenth Century West Indian Creole Experience', *Caribbean Quarterly*, Vol. 36, nos. 1 and 2 (June 1990) pp 16–39.
3. Jane Robinson, *Mary Seacole: The Charismatic Black Nurse Who Became a Heroine of the Crimea* (Constable, London: 2005) p 7.
4. Rene Chartrand, *British Forces in the West Indies 1793 – 1815* (Osprey, London: 1996) p 3.
5. *Adventures*, p 4.
6. Ziggi Alexander and Audrey Dewjee, *Mary Seacole. Jamaican National Heroine and 'Doctress' in the Crimean War* (Brent Library Service, London: 1982) p 3.
7. Chartrand, *British Forces in the West Indies*, p 3.
8. Thomas Dancer, *The Medical Assistant; or Jamaican Practice of Physic. Designed Chiefly for the Use of Families and Plantations* (Alexander Aikman, Kingston, Jamaica: 1801) p v.
9. Sir Nicholas Harris Nicolas (ed), *Dispatches and Letters of Vice-Admiral Lord Viscount Nelson* (Colburn, London: 1844–6) Vol 1, p 34; Christopher Hibbert, *Nelson. A Personal History* (Penguin, London: 1995) p 28; John Bigelow, *Jamaica in 1850* (Putnam, New York: 1851).
10. *Adventures*, pp 2–3.
11. Robinson, *Mary Seacole*, p 18.
12. *Adventures*, p 4.
13. See Ron Ramdin, *The Making of the Black Working Class in Britain* (Wildwood House, Aldershot: 1987), and Peter Fryer, *Staying Power. The History of Black People in Britain* (Pluto Press, London: 1984).
14. Ramdin, *The Making of the Black Working Class*, pp 25–8.
15. *Adventures*, p 14.
16. *Adventures*, p 5.
17. Robinson, *Mary Seacole*, pp 30–2.
18. Alexander and Dewjee, *Jamaican National Heroine and 'Doctress' in the Crimean War*, p 3.
19. *Adventures*, pp 5–6.
20. 'To the Reader' in *Adventures*, pp vii–viii.
21. *Adventures*, p 7.
22. *Adventures*, p 11.
23. *Adventures*, pp 10–11.
24. *Adventures*, p 14.
25. *Adventures*, pp 18–19.
26. *Adventures*, pp 24–5.
27. *Adventures*, p 27.
28. *Adventures*, p 30.
29. *Adventures*, p 34.
30. *Adventures*, pp 36–7.
31. *Adventures*, p 38.
32. Robinson, *Mary Seacole*, p 66.
33. *Adventures*, pp 42–3.
34. *Adventures*, pp 47–8.
35. *Adventures*, p 50.
36. *Adventures*, pp 57–8.
37. *Adventures*, p 60.
38. *Adventures*, p 63.
39. *Adventures*, pp 65–6.

40. *Adventures*, p 68
41. *The Times*, 23 December 1853.
42. Alexander and Dewjee, *Jamaica National Heroine and 'Doctress' in the Crimean War*, p 6.
43. *Adventures*, p 73.
44. *Adventures*, pp 74–5.
45. *Adventures*, p 76
46. *Adventures*, p 77.
47. *Adventures*, p 78.
48. *Adventures*, p 79
49. *Adventures*, p 80.
50. *Adventures*, p 81.
51. *Adventures*, p 84.
52. *Adventures*, p 87.
53. *Adventures*, p 89.
54. *Adventures*, pp 90–1.
55. *Adventures*, pp 90–4.
56. *Adventures*, pp 96–7.
57. *Adventures*, pp 98–101.
58. *Adventures*, pp 105–6, 108.
59. Paul Kerr *et al*, *The Crimean War* (Boxtree, London: 1997), pp 9–10.
60. Kerr *et al*, *The Crimean War*, pp 13–15.
61. Piers Compton, *Colonel's Lady & Camp Follower: The Story of Women in The Crimean War* (Robert Hale & Company, London: 1970), p 18.
62. Compton, *Colonel's Lady & Camp Follower*, pp 18–32.
63. Compton, *Colonel's Lady & Camp Follower*, pp 18–32
64. Compton, *Colonel's Lady & Camp Follower*, pp 15–32; see also Christopher Hibbert, *The Destruction of Lord Raglan* (Longman, London: 1961).
65. *Adventures*, pp 109–11.
66. *Adventures*, p 114.
67. *Adventures*, p 119.
68. *Adventures*, pp 121, 123.
69. *Adventures*, pp 140–1.
70. *Adventures*, pp 143–4.
71. *Adventures*, p 146.
72. *Adventures*, pp 124–5.
73. *Punch*, 6 December 1856.
74. *Adventures*, pp 126–8.
75. *Adventures*, pp 146–7.
76. *Adventures*, p 148.
77. Alexis Soyer, (eds M Barthorp and E Ray), *A Culinary Campaign* (Southover Press, Lewes: 1995) p 142.
78. Soyer, *A Culinary Campaign*, p 143.
79. *Adventures*, p 149.
80. *Adventures*, pp 151–4.
81. *Adventures*, p 154–5.
82. *Adventures*, pp 155–8.
83. *Adventures*, pp 160–2.
84. *Adventures*, pp 163–4, 166.
85. *Adventures*, pp 168–71.
86. *The Times*, 11 April 1857.
87. *Adventures*, pp 168–176.
88. *Adventures*, pp 178–9.
89. *Adventures*, pp 183–7.
90. *Adventures*, pp 189–94.
91. Robinson, *Mary Seacole*, p 156.
92. *News of the World*, 31 August 1856.
93. *The Times*, 26 August 1856.
94. *Punch*, 25 October 1856.
95. *The Times*, 7 November 1856.
96. *Punch*, 6 December 1856.
97. Robinson, *Mary Seacole*, p 167.
98. See W H Russell, quoted at beginning of *Adventures*.
99. Robinson, *Mary Seacole*, p 173.
100. Claydon House Trust Collection, MS/9004/60. Quoted in Robinson, *Mary Seacole*, p 191.
101. Helen Rappaport, 'The Invitation that Never Came: Mary Seacole After the Crimea', *History Today*, Vol. 55 (2005), pp 9–15.
102. Robinson, *Mary Seacole*, p 155; Rappaport, 'The Invitation that Never Came', pp 9–15.
103. *Adventures*, p 66.
104. *Adventures*, p 8.
105. *Adventures*, pp 80–1.
106. *Adventures*, p 74.
107. Robinson, *Mary Seacole*, pp 197–8.

Chronology

Year	Date	Life
1805		Born in Kingston, Jamaica.
1807	2	African slave trade in British territories abolished.
1822	17	? First visit to London.
1823	18	Second visit to London.
1826	21	Mary reaches age of majority.
1836	31	Marries Edwin Horatio Hamilton Seacole, an Englishman.
1843	38	Her house in Kingston is destroyed in a fire.

Year	History	Culture
1805	Battle of Trafalgar: Admiral Lord Nelson killed. Battle of Austerlitz.	Scott, *Lay of the Last Minstrel*. Beethoven, opera *Fidelio*.
1807	Treaty of Tilsit between Napoleon, the Tsar and the King of Prussia.	Byron, *Hours of Idleness*. Beethoven, *Leonora Overture No. 3*.
1822	Greek independence proclaimed. Louis Pasteur born.	Schubert's Symphony No. 8 in B minor ('The Unfinished'). Pushkin, *Eugene Onegin*.
1823	Declaration of the Monroe Doctrine by the USA. First publication of British medical journal *The Lancet*.	Beethoven's *Missa Solemnis*.
1826	Foundation of University College, London. Russian ultimatum to the Ottoman Empire over Serbia.	James Fenimore Cooper, *The Last of the Mohicans*. Mendelssohn, Overture to 'A Midsummer Night's Dream'.
1836	Chartist Movement in Britain demands universal suffrage. Battle of the Alamo, Texas.	Dickens, *The Pickwick Papers*. Mayerbeer, opera *Les Huguenots*.
1843	Maori revolts against Britain in New Zealand. Marc Brunel's Thames Tunnel opened.	Tennyson, *Morte d'Arthur*. Wagner, opera *The Flying Dutchman*.

Year	Date	Life
1844	39	Edwin Seacole dies.
1850	45	Cholera outbreak in Kingston. Mary travels to Panama to work with her brother and opens her 'Independent Hotel.'
1853	48	Returns to Jamaica, where there is a severe outbreak of yellow fever.
1854	49	Arrives in London. Goes to the Crimea: meets Florence Nightingale.
1855	50	Opens her British Hotel in the Crimea. Meets the famous French chef Alexis Soyer.
1856	51	Leaves the Crimea.
1857	52	Publication of her autobiography Wonderful *Adventures of Mrs Seacole in Many Lands*. Fund-raising concerts in her honour at Royal Surrey Gardens. Sculpted by Count Gleichen.

Year	History	Culture
1844	Karl Marx meets Friedrich Engels in Paris. First use of Morse's electric telegraph.	Dumas père, *The Count of Monte Cristo*. Turner, painting *Rain, Steam and Speed*.
1850	Anglo-Kaffir war in South Africa. Stephenson's cast-iron railway bridge over the Tyne at Newcastle opened.	Hawthorne, *The Scarlet Letter*. Wagner, opera *Lohengrin*.
1853	Outbreak of war between Russia and the Ottoman Empire. Compulsory smallpox vaccination in Britain.	Charlotte Brönte, *Villette*. Verdi, operas *Il Trovatore* and *La Traviata*.
1854	Britain and France ally with the Ottoman Empire and declare war on Russia (the Crimean War).	Tennyson, poem *The Charge of the Light Brigade*.
1855	Electric telegraph established between London and Balaclava in the Crimea. Russians surrender in the Crimea.	Dickens, *Little Dorrit*. Trollope, *The Warden*.
1856	Queen Victoria institutes the Victoria Cross. Peace conference in Paris recognises the integrity of the Ottoman Empire.	Flaubert, *Madame Bovary*.
1857	Outbreak of the Indian Mutiny. Tsar Alexander II begins emancipation of Russian serfs.	Baudelaire, *Les Fleurs du Mal*. Thomas Hughes, *Tom Brown's Schooldays*.

Year	Date	Life
1858	53	Her autobiography reprinted.
1859	54	Returns to Jamaica.
1865	60	Morant Bay Rebellion in Jamaica. The local militia kills 28 civilians and British Governor Edward Eyre orders that the leader of the riots, Paul Bogle, be hanged.
1866	61	Her portrait is painted in oils by Charles Challen.
1867	62	Seacole Fund resurrected in London.
1870	65	Returns to England. Seeks to go as a nurse to the Franco-Prussian War, but is refused permission.
1881	76	Dies 'a rich woman' and is laid to rest in Kensal Rise Cemetery.

Year	History	Culture
1858	End of the Indian Mutiny. First meeting of the General Medical Council, London.	William P Frith, painting *Derby Day*.
1859	Construction of Suez Canal begins (to 1869). Franco-Austrian War.	Dickens, *A Tale of Two Cities*. Verdi, opera *Un Ballo in Maschera*.
1865	End of the American Civil War. Thirteenth Amendment to US Constitution abolishes slavery.	Lewis Carroll, *Alice's Adventures in Wonderland*. Wagner, opera *Tristan und Isolde*.
1866	Austro-Prussian War.	Dostoyevsky, *Crime and Punishment*.
1867	British Parliamentary Reform Act.	Zola, *Thérèse Raquin*. Johann Strauss II, waltz *The Blue Danube*.
1870	Outbreak of the Franco-Prussian War. Death of Confederate general Robert E Lee.	Jules Verne, *Twenty Thousand Leagues under the Sea*. Delibes, ballet *Coppélia*.
1881	First Anglo-Boer War. Flogging abolished in British armed forces.	Henry James, *Portrait of a Lady*. Monet, painting *Sunshine and Snow*.

Further Reading

Autobiography

Seacole, Mary, *Wonderful Adventures of Mary Seacole in Many Lands* (James Blackwood, London: 1858).

_____, (eds. Z Alexander and A Dewjee), *Wonderful Adventures . . .* (Falling Wall Press, London: 1984).

_____, (ed W Andrews), *Wonderful Adventures . . .* (Oxford University Pres, New York: 1988).

Published Primary Sources

Bigelow, John, *Jamaica in 1850* (Putnam, New York: 1851).

Blackwood, Lady Alicia, *A Narrative of Personal Experiences . . . Through the Crimean War* (Hatchards, London: 1881).

British Army, *Local Regulations and Orders for the Troops Serving in the West India Command and Her Majesty's Colonies on the South American Continent* (London: 1843).

Buchanan, George, *Camp Life. As Seen by a Civilian* (Maclehose, Glasgow: 1871).

Buzzard, Thomas, *With the Turkish Army in the Crimea and Asia Minor* (John Murray, London: 1915).

Campbell, Colin Frederick, *Letters from Camp* (Bentley, London: 1894).

Carlyle, Thomas, *Occasional Discourse on the Nigger Question* (Bosworth, London: 1853).

Carmichael, Mrs, *Domestic Manners and Social Conditions of the White, Coloured and Negro Population of the West Indies* (Whittaker and Treacher, London: 1833).

Clifford, Henry, *His Letters and Sketches from the Crimea* (Michael Joseph, London: 1956).

Dancer, Thomas, *The Medical Assistant; or Jamaican Practice of Physic. Designed Chiefly for the Use of Families and Plantations* (Alexander Aikman, Kingston, Jamaica: 1801).

Duberly, Fanny, *Journal Kept During the Russian War . . .* (Longman, London: 1855).

Edgerton, Robert, *Daguerian Excursions in Jamaica* (A Duperly, Kingston, Jamaica: n.d).

Equiano, Olaudah, *The Interesting Narrative of the Life . . .* 2 vols (London: 1789).

Fabens, Joseph W, *A Story of Life on the Isthmus* (Putnam, New York: 1853).

Falconbridge, Ann Maria, *Narrative of Two voyages to the River Sierra Leone during the Years 1791-2-3 . . . Also the Present State of the Slave Trade in the West Indies and the Improbability of its Total Abolition* (Higham, London: 1802).

Galt, Edwin, *The Camp and the Cutter; or A Cruise to the Crimea* (Hodgson, London: 1856).

Goodman, Margaret, *Experiences of an English Sister of Mercy* (Smith, Elder, London: 1862).

Griswold, C D, *The Isthmus of Panama and What I Saw There* (Dewitt and Davenport, New York: 1852).

Handbook of Jamaica . . . by Two Members of the Jamaican Civil Service (Kingston: Jamaica Government Printing Establishment, 1881).

Hornby, Lady, *Constantinople during the Crimean War* (Pall Mall Press, London: 1971).

Kelly, Mrs. Tom, *From the Fleet in the Fifties* (Hurst and Blackett, London: 1902).

Montez, Lola, *Autobiography and Lectures* (James Blackwood, London: 1858).

Nelson, Admiral Lord Horatio, *The Letters of Lord Nelson and Lady Hamilton* (Thomas Lovewell, London: 1814).

Nicolas, Sir Nicholas Harris (ed), *Dispatches and Letters of Vice-Admiral Lord Viscount Nelson* (Colburn, London: 1844–6).

Nugent, Lady Maria (ed. Philip Wright), *Lady Nugent's Journal of Her Residence in Jamaica from 1801–1805* (Institute of Jamaica, Kingston, Jamaica: 1966).

Prince, Mary, *The History of Mary Prince: A West Indian Slave related by Herself* (Westleigh and Davis, London; Waugh and Innis, Edinburgh: 1831).

Reid, Douglas Arthur, *Memories of the Crimean War* (St. Catherine's Press, London: 1911).

Robins, Major Colin, *Captain Dunscombe's Diary: The Real Crimean War* (Withycut House, Bowdon: 2003).

Russell, Sir William Howard (ed N Bentley), *Russell's Despatches from the Crimea 1854–1856* (Deutsch, London: 1996).

Simpson, William, *The Seat of the War in the East from Eighty-one Drawings made During the War in the Crimea* (Day and Son, London: 1902).

_____, (ed G Eyre-Todd) *The Autobiography of William Simpson RI* (T. Fisher Unwin, London: 1903).

Soyer, Alexis, (eds M Barthorp and E Ray), *A Culinary Campaign* (Southover Press, Lewes: 1995).

Terrot, Sarah Anne (ed. R G Richardson), *Nurse Sarah Anne. With Florence Nightingale at Scutari* (John Murray, London: 1977).

Vicars, Captain Hedley (ed C Marsh), Memorials . . . (James Nisbet, London: 1856).

Vieth, Frederick, *Recollections of the Crimean Campaign* (John Lovell, Montreal: 1907).

Secondary Sources

Alexander, Ziggi, and Audrey Dewjee, *Mary Seacole. Jamaican National Heroine and 'Doctress' in the Crimean War* (Brent Library Service, London: 1982).

Ayensu, E, *Medicinal Plants of the West Indies* (Reference Publications, Algonac: 1981).

Backhouse, Francis (ed), *Women of the Klondike* (White Cap, Vancouver: 1995).

Baker, Christopher, *Jamaica* (Lonely Planet, London: 2000).

Bolt, Christine, *Victorian Attitudes to Race* (Routledge and Keegan Paul, London: 1971).

Braithwaite, Edward, *The Development of Creole Society in Jamaica 1770–1820* (Clarendon Press, Oxford: 1971).

Briggs, Asa, *Victorian People 1851–1867* (Chicago University Press, Chicago: 1970).

Brooke, Elisabeth, *Women Healers through History* (Women's Press, London: 1993).

Carnegie, M E, 'Black Nurses at the Front,' *American Journal of Nursing*, Vol. 84 (1984).

Bonham Carter, Violet (ed), *Surgeon in the Crimea* (Michael Joseph, London: 1956).

Chartrand, Rene, *British Forces in the West Indies 1793–1815* (Osprey, London: 1996).

Coleman, Terry, *Nelson* (Bloomsbury, London: 2001).

Compton, Piers, *Colonel's Lady and Camp Follower. The Story of Women in the Crimean War* (Hale, London: 1970).

Cook, E, *The Life of Florence Nightingale* (Macmillan, London: 1914).

Cooper, Helen, 'England: The Imagined Community of Aurora Leigh and Mrs. Seacole', *Studies in Browning and His Circle*, Vol 20 (1993).

Crawford, P, 'The Other Lady With the Lamp', *Nursing Times*, Vol 88, no 11 (1992).

Delany, A, *A History of the Catholic Church in Jamaica* (Jesuit Press, New York: 1930).

Edwards, Paul, and David Dabydeen (eds), *Black Writers in Britain 1760–1890* (Edinburgh: Edinburgh University Press, 1991).

Ffrench-Blake, R, *The Crimean War* (Cooper, London: 1971).

File, Nigel, and Chris Power, *Black Settlers in Britain 1555–1958* (Heinemann, London: 1981).

Fish, Cheryl, *Black and White Women's Travel Narratives* (University Press of Florida, Gainesville: 2004).

Fletcher, Ian and Natalia Ischenko, *The Crimean War: A Clash of Empires* (Spellmount, Staplehurst: 2004).

Fraser, Flora, *Beloved Emma. The Life of Emma, Lady Hamilton* (Wiedenfeld and Nicholson, London: 1994).

Frederick, Rhona, 'Creole Performance in *Wonderful Adventures of Mrs. Seacole in Many Lands*', Gender and History, Vol 15, no 3 (2004).

Fryer, Peter, *Staying Power. The History of Black People in Britain* (Pluto Press, London: 1984).

Gernsheim, Helmut and Alison, *Roger Fenton: Photographer of the Crimean War* (Secker and Warburg, London: 1954).

Gerzina, Gretchen, *Black England. Life Before Emancipation* (John Murray, London: 1995).

Gikaandi, Simon, *Maps of Englishness. Writing Identity in the Culture of Colonialism* (Columbia University Press, New York: 1996).

Golby, J M, *Culture and Society in Britain 1850–1890* (Oxford University Press, Oxford: 1986).

Goldie, Sue, *Calendar of the Letters of Florence Nightingale* (Oxford Microforms, Oxford: 1983).

_____(ed), '*I Have Done My Duty': Florence Nightingale in the Crimean War 1854–1856* (Manchester University Press, Manchester: 1987).

Gustafson, M, 'Mary Seacole, the Florence Nightingale of Jamaica,' *Christian Nurse International*, Vol 12, no 4 (1996).

Hawthorn, Evelyn, 'Self-Writing, Literary Traditions and Post-Emancipation Identity: the Case of Mary Seacole', *Biography*, Vol 23, no 2 (2000).

Henriques, Fernando, *Children of Caliban: Miscegenation* (Secker and Warburg, London: 1964).

Hibbert, Christopher, *The Destruction of Lord Raglan* (Longman, London: 1961).

_____ , *Nelson. A Personal History* (Penguin, London: 1995).

Hume, Hamilton, *The Life of Edward John Eyre, Late Governor of Jamaica* (Bentley, London: 1867).

Hurwitz, Samuel and Edith, *Jamaica. A Historical Portrait* (Pall Mall Press, London: 1971).

Innes, C L, *A History of Black and Asian Writing in Britain, 1700-2000* (Cambridge University Press, Cambridge: 1992).

Iveson-Iveson, J, 'The Forgotten Heroine', *Nursing Mirror*, Vol 157 (1983).

Josephs, Aleric, 'Mary Seacole: Jamaican Nurse and "Doctress"', *Jamaican Historical Review*, Vol 17 (1991).

Judd, Catherine, *Bedside Seductions. Nursing and the Victorian Imagination 1830–1880* (Macmillan, London: 1998).

Kerr, Paul *et al*, *The Crimean War* (Boxtree, London: 1997).

Khan, H, 'Remembering Mary Seacole', *West Indian Digest* (June 1981).

King, A, 'Mary Seacole,' *Essence*, Vol 4, nos 11 and 12 (1974).

Kinglake, A W, *The Invasion of the Crimea* (Blackwood, Edinburgh: 1863–87).

Laguerre, Michel, *Afro-Caribbean Folk Medicine* (Bergin and Garvey, South Hadley: 1987).

Long, Edward, *The History of Jamaica* (Cass, London: 1970).

Lorimer, Douglas, *Colour, Class and the Victorians. English Attitudes to the Negro in the Mid-Nineteenth Century* (Leicester University Press, Leicester: 1978).

Malam, John, *Tell Me More About Pioneers: Mary Seacole* (Evans, London: 1999).

McKenna, Bernard, 'Fancies of Exclusive Possession: Validation and Dissociation in Mary Seacole's England and Caribbean', *Philological Quarterly*, Vol 76, no 2 (1997).

Messmer, P R, and Y Parchment, 'Mary Grant Seacole: The first Nurse Practitioner', *Clinical Excellence for Nurse Practitioners*, Vol 2, no 1 (1998).

Mills, Therese, *Great West Indians* (Longman Carribean, Kingston: 1973).

Moorcroft, Christine, and Magnus Magnusson: *Famous People: Mary Seacole 1805–1881* (Channel 4, London: 1998).

Moore, Henry Charles, *Noble Deeds of the World's Heroines* (Religious Tract Society, London: 1903).

Morris, Helen, *Portrait of a Chef* (Oxford University Press, Oxford: 1980).

Nettleford, Rex, 'Freedom of Thought and Experience: Nineteenth Century West Indian Creole Experience', *Caribbean Quarterly*, Vol. 36, nos. 1 and 2 (June 1990).

Paquet, Sandra Pouchon, 'Mary Seacole: The Enigma of Arrival', *African American Review*, Vol 26, no 4 (1992).

Pollitt, N, 'Forgotten Heroine', *Times Higher Educational Supplement*, no 3965 (1992).

Pritchard, R E (ed): *Dickens's England. Life in Victorian Times* (Sutton, Stroud: 2002).

Rappaport, Helen, 'The Invitation that Never Came: Mary Seacole After the Crimea,' *History Today*, Vol 55 (February 2005), pp 9–15.

Ramdin, Ron, *The Making of the Black Working Class in Britain* (Wildwood House, Aldershot: 1987).

——————, *Reimaging Britain: 500 Years of Black and Asian History* (Pluto Press, London: 1999).

Robinson, Amy, 'Authority and the Public Display of Identity: *Wonderful Adventures of Mrs. Seacole in Many Lands*', *Feminist Studies*, Vol 20, no 3 (1994).

Robinson, Jane, *Wayward Women: A Guide to Women Travellers* (Oxford University Press, Oxford: 1990).

——————, *Mary Seacole: The Charismatic Black Nurse Who*

Became a Heroine of the Crimea (Constable, London: 2005).

Scobie, James, *Black Britannia: A History of Blacks in Britain* (Johnson Publishing, Chicago: 1972).

Seymour, Bruce, *Lola Montez. A Life* (Yale University Press, New Haven: 1996).

Shepherd, John, *The Crimean Doctors. A History of the British Medical Services in the Crimean War* (Liverpool University Press, Liverpool: 1991).

Sheridan, Richard, *Doctors and Slaves. A Medical and Demographic History of Slavery in the British West Indies 1680–1834* (Cambridge University Press, Cambridge: 1985).

Shyllon, F O, *Black People in Britain, 1555–1833* (Institute of Race Relations/Oxford University Press, London: 1977).

Small, Hugh, *Florence Nightingale: Avenging Angel* (Constable, London: 1998).

Smith, J P, 'Mary Jane Seacole', *Journal of Advanced Nursing*, Vol 9, no 5 (1984).

Summers, Anne, *Angels and Citizens. British Women as Military Nurses 1854–1914* (Routledge and Keegan Paul, London: 1988).

Sweetman, John, *The Crimean War* (Osprey, Oxford: 2001).

Tisdall, E E P, *Mrs. Duberly's Campaigns* (Jarrolds, London: 1963).

Vernon, C, 'The Story of Mary Seacole', *Jamaican Nurse*, Vol 25 (1986).

Vulliamy, C, *Crimea. The Campaign of 1854-56* (Cape, London: 1939).

Walvin, James, *Black and White: The Negro and English Society, 1555–1945* (Allen Lane, the Penguin Press, London: 1973).

Woodham Smith, Cecil, *Florence Nightingale 1820–1910* (Constable, London: 1950)

Picture Sources

The author and publishers wish to express their thanks to the following sources of illustrative material and/or permission to reproduce it. They will make proper acknowledgements in future editions in the event that any ommissions have occurred.

Ann Ronan Picture Library/HIP/Topfoto: pp. 50, 53, 90, 103; Courtesy of Helen Rappaport/ National Portrait Gallery, London: pp. vi, 124, 125; Mary Evans Picture Library: pp. i, ii, 69, 81, 118, 119; Topham picturepoint: pp. 2, 7, 11, 16, 18, 33, 39, 56, 63, 66, 73, 86, 96, 100, 101, 104, 113, 116, Topham Picturepoint/Roger Viollet: pp. 61, 72, 83.

Index

Alexander the Great
by Nigel Cawthorne
'moves through the career at a brisk,
dependable canter in his pocket
biography for Haus.'
BOYD TONKIN, *The Independent*
ISBN 1-904341-56-X (pb) £9.99

Armstrong
by David Bradbury
'it is a fine and well-researched
introduction'
GEORGE MELLY *Daily Mail*
ISBN 1-904341-46-2 (pb) £8.99

Bach
by Martin Geck
'The production values of the book
are exquisite.' *Guardian*
ISBN 1-904341-16-0 (pb) £8.99
ISBN 1-904341-35-7 (hb) £12.99

Beethoven
by Martin Geck
'...this little gem is a truly handy
reference.' *Musical Opinion*
ISBN 1-904341-00-4 (pb) £8.99
ISBN 1-904341-03-9 (hb) £12.99

Bette Davis
by Laura Moser
'The author compellingly unearths
the complex, self-destructive woman
that lay beneath the steely persona
of one of the best-loved actresses of
all time.'
ISBN 1-904341-48-9 (pb) £9.99

Bevan
by Clare Beckett
and Francis Beckett
"Haus, the enterprising new
imprint, adds another name to its
list of short biographies ... a timely
contribution.'
GREG NEALE, *BBC History*
ISBN 1-904341-63-2 (pb) £9.99

Brahms
by Hans A Neunzig
'These handy volumes fill a gap in
the market for readable,
comprehensive and attractively
priced biographies admirably.'
JULIAN HAYLOCK, *Classic fm*
ISBN 1-904341-17-9 (pb) £8.99

Gershwin
by Ruth Leon
'Musical theatre aficionados will relish
Ruth Leon's GERSHWIN, a succinct
but substantial account of the great composer's
life'
MICHAEL ARDITTI, *The Independent*
ISBN 1-904341-23-3 (pb) £9.99

Johnson
by Timothy Wilson Smith
'from a prize-winning author a biography
of the famous and perennially fascinating
figure, Samuel Johnson'
ISBN 1-904341-81-0 (pb) £9.99

Joyce
by Ian Pindar
'I enjoyed the book very much, and
much approve of this skilful kind of pop-
ularisation. It reads wonderfully well.'
TERRY EAGLETON
ISBN 1-904341-58-6 (pb) £9.99

Kafka
by Klaus Wagenbach
'one of the most useful books on Kafka
ever published.' New Scientist
ISBN 1-904341-01-2 (hb) £12.99
ISBN 1-904341-02-0 (pb) £8.99